DOING
NATURALISTIC
INQUIRY

DOING NATURALISTIC INQUIRY

A Guide to Methods

David A. Erlandson
Edward L. Harris
Barbara L. Skipper
Steve D. Allen

SAGE Publications
International Educational and Professional Publisher
Newbury Park   London   New Delhi

For information address:

SAGE Publications, Inc.
2455 Teller Road
Newbury Park, California 91320

SAGE Publications Ltd.
6 Bonhill Street
London EC2A 4PU
United Kingdom

SAGE Publications India Pvt. Ltd.
M-32 Market
Greater Kailash I
New Delhi 110 048 India

Printed in the United States of America

Library of Congress Cataloging-in-Publication Data

Doing naturalistic inquiry : a guide to methods / David A. Erlandson
    . . . [et al.].
        p.   cm.
    Includes bibliographical references and index.
    ISBN 0-8039-4937-5. — ISBN 0-8039-4938-3 (pbk.)
    1. Social sciences—Methodology. 2. Paradigms (Social sciences)
I. Erlandson, David A.
H61.D62   1993
300'.72—dc20   93-3651

93   94   95   96   10   9   8   7   6   5   4   3   2   1

Sage Production Editor: Megan M. McCue

Contents

Foreword

ALTERNATIVE PARADIGMS—that is, sets of beliefs that lead to ways of approaching inquiry that are essentially different from the historically correct "received" paradigm—have been recognized for well over a decade. But the literature that deals with these alternatives has been long on theory and short on practical procedural suggestions (I suppose I must declare myself guilty of that neglect as much as anyone). I welcome this book by David Erlandson and his colleagues precisely because it is an effort to deal with the "how to do it" aspect of at least one such alternative—naturalistic inquiry (which I would now prefer to call "constructivist inquiry")—and to do so not by prescriptive formulas but by lessons and examples drawn (mostly) from their own work.

Despite its deceptively simple appearance, this book is not an easy read. There are several problems in dealing with paradigm distinctions to which the reader must remain constantly alert to prevent misinterpretations and misconstructions of the book's content. Please bear with me as I enumerate such conceptual stumbling blocks. For each I will direct attention to particular places in the book that are especially relevant, but the reader must realize that these problems pervade the material (in this book as they would in any book dealing with paradigm distinctions) and will catch the reader unawares unless special attention is given to them.

1. *Naturalistic inquiry is not equivalent to qualitative inquiry.* The reader should not confuse naturalistic inquiry with qualitative inquiry—that is, inquiry utilizing only qualitative methods. Although a strong case can be made for the proposition that qualitative methods have certain strengths that are worth utilizing in any study regardless of the inquiry paradigm that guides it, that case is not equivalent to the *paradigm-level* case that can be made in favor of naturalistic inquiry (or any other alternative form of inquiry). Studies that are based exclusively on qualitative methods but designed in terms of positivist assumptions remain positivist studies. Naturalistic studies, while they may include quantitative methods, are *essentially different*; that difference has nothing whatever to do with the issues (if there be such) of qualitative versus quantitative methods. This theme is developed in both Chapters 1 and 2.

2. *The naturalistic paradigm is incommensurable with the conventional paradigm.* The reader should bear in mind that one cannot fairly understand any paradigm, naturalistic or otherwise, on the basis of considerations evolved in relation to some other paradigm; to do so would be equivalent to judging, say, Roman Catholic theology on the basis of Lutheran dogma (or vice versa). The naturalistic paradigm is *incommensurable* with positivism in the same way that the notions of flat earth and round earth are conceptually incommensurable. By "incommensurable" is meant that no common points of reference exist to which differences and conflicts among paradigms may be submitted for resolution. It is the basic problem of reductionism that it assumes just such common points. The reader must constantly resist the temptation to call naturalistic inquiry to account in positivist terms (or vice versa, for that matter). This point should be clear after reading Chapter 2.

3. *The underdeveloped state of alternative paradigms.* The reader must always bear in mind that alternative paradigms remain as yet largely underdeveloped; there are many conceptual and practical gaps. That should not be surprising; conventional science (positivism) has had some 400 years to lift itself by argumentation and experience to its present sophisticated level, while its alternatives have had—by any stretch of the imagination—less than a century. Indeed, the need for a "new" paradigm in social research is only now becoming apparent (see Chapter 1).

Dr. Yvonna Lincoln, my frequent collaborator, and I have hoped that practical books such as this one would emerge to help remedy that situation. Even though they might be halting and incomplete in some sense, reflecting that alternative paradigms are still in the process of becoming, they could nevertheless provide the *grounding in experience* that would simultaneously test the theory while demonstrating practical ways to manage the "new" inquiry. We have always contended that constructions can and should change as new information accrues and sophistication increases; we reserve the right, we have argued, to "get smarter." If much remains murky, well, that is less a reason to condemn this or any other similar book's shortcomings than to sound a tocsin for other work that will illuminate what remains to be explored. (Many areas still to be explored are discussed in a large number of the books and articles listed in the reference section.)

4. *The lingering effect of ingrained conventional presuppositions.* Many of this book's readers will come to it dragging a heavy baggage of conventional presuppositions; after all, were we not all raised by our intellectual forebears to believe that positivism was the "true" way to knowledge? For example, most positivists assume that there is some way that things actually "are" and actually "work" (a concrete reality and its mechanisms) and that science can find out what those are: That objectivity in inquiry is mandated and, to the extent that inquiry is objective, it will de facto be value-free; that the aim of science is to arrive at generalizations, preferably causal, whose "truth" is determined by how well they enable prediction and control; and the like. In contrast, most proponents of naturalistic inquiry assume, again for example, that the ways things are constructed to be and to work depends on the particular human constructor entertaining the ideas (in other words, that there are multiple realities rather than a single reality, each relative to the constructors' experience); that subjective inquiry is the only kind possible to do and that as a result all studies will be value-influenced to an indeterminate degree; that the aim of inquiry is the development of shared constructions (including constructions for action) among members of a particular group, society, or culture, and that if others wish to learn from the given inquiry, they do so chiefly through the "vicarious experience" that a good case study report provides; and so on.

One major message of this book is that the conventional construction about the meaning and aim of inquiry is only one of many possible constructions and that this particular construction—the "received view"—is being rejected by many in favor of other possible constructions or paradigms. One of these other paradigms is naturalistic inquiry. It should be noted that while adherents of alternative paradigms can typically accept the conventional positivist view as one of the useful (if somewhat dated) paradigms that have been proposed over the years (indeed, one that has resulted in some remarkable gains for society), adherents of the conventional view seem to be unable to accept alternative paradigms with similar

DOING NATURALISTIC INQUIRY

equanimity. As Hannah Arendt has noted, "Truth is coercive." If science is believed to produce findings about the way things *really are* and *really work*, then formulations challenging its views must be regarded as inherently in error (if not fomented by the devil). Chapter 2 sheds light on this debate.

5. *The hidden traps of our language and culture.* In a similar vein, the reader must remain aware that the very structure of our language (and thus our conceptual structure?) heavily depends on the traditional terms of positivism, which have been deeply ingrained within us from early childhood on. It is particularly hard to expunge from our memories such terms as *causality*, *generalization*, *objectivity*, *bias*, and the like; these concepts do not apply to naturalistic inquiry. Their absence from among the elements discussed is a virtue, not a vice, from the naturalistic point of view.

Consider bias as an example. As normally used, *bias* implies a distortion from the way things really are or work. The distortion may be conscious or unconscious. Often the latter point is made; it is an easy way to undermine an opponent who disagrees with you to argue that he himself is unaware of the biases he carries. Bias is a serious problem in positivism precisely because it postulates that there is a way that things really are and really work; to perceive them in other ways is a clear case of bias, that is, of distortion. But the naturalist would say only that some other individual merely has a different construction from his or her own. The point is to determine *why* these differences exist; it may, for example, be a simple case of one or the other lacking relevant information or not being sufficiently sophisticated to weigh and interpret the information that is available. It may be a case of one or the other construction being based on misinformation that can be corrected. It may, of course, also be a case that one of the constructors (perhaps even the inquirer?) deliberately misleads the other for the sake of some hidden agenda or provides disinformation to that end. But even in this case the naturalist would not claim bias, but only premeditated deception. Such situations would be judged on ethical or moral grounds, not on the grounds of bias (the deceiver *knows* that a misconstruction is being offered). The lesson from all this? That what appear to be missing terms are perhaps absent because conceptually they have no place within the naturalistic paradigm, rather than because they have been overlooked by the authors.

Or consider as another example the concept of *variable*. The first question often asked of a doctoral student laying out a proposed dissertation before a research committee is "What are your independent and dependent variables?" The implication: How can inquiry be conceptualized (designed) unless the inquirer is clear about the variables to be involved? This strong affinity for the concept of variable may lead the unwary reader to presume, for example, that *context* or *culture*, as these terms are used by Erlandson, Harris, Skipper, and Allen, are nothing more than variables themselves (consider how the term *culture* has been interpreted in management or leadership literature as just another variable that the alert administrator can manipulate to organizational ends). But such a shallow interpretation misses the view of culture as a well-understood, accepted, and shared construction that sets the context for all human activity within its bounds. It is even the case that authors writing books about alternative paradigms will themselves unwittingly allow such meanings to creep in, so deeply ingrained are they. (Try getting along for a day without ever uttering the word *variable* or any of its synonyms to get some sense of the difficulty involved in cleansing the mind of inappropriate constructions.) But the reader should not be misled by these aberrations; when they occur, they are likely to be oversights, not assertions of principle. Chapter 2 takes up this problem of language in considerable depth.

6. *Each paradigm has its own appropriate rule and criteria.* The reader must not assume that the traditional rules for guiding (positivists would say, designing) inquiry, or assessing its quality, fairly and equally apply to inquiries conducted within the presuppositions of any alternative paradigm. Validity, for example, often interpreted as the extent of isomorphism between the findings and the reality they are supposed to represent, can have little meaning when the realities are multiple in nature and exist only in people's minds. Each paradigm's assumptions are also father to its own appropriate rules and criteria. The state of affairs constitutes another major message that this book endeavors to make clear, even while offering tentative (in process of becoming) rules more clearly consonant with the propositions that undergird this particular alternative. The "rules" of naturalistic inquiry are found in some detail in Chapters 3, 4, 5, and 6; quality criteria are introduced in Chapter 2 and elaborated in detail in Chapter 7.

7. *The processes of carrying out naturalistic inquiry are not the same as the processes for carrying out conventional inquiry.* The reader ought not to assume that the naturalistic process of research will include the same elements as would conventional research. Much is made of this fact in Chapters 5 and 6. For example, it is not possible to specify the "design" elements for a naturalistic study a priori (they must emerge as the study unfolds), nor is it possible (largely) to specify needed instrumentation a priori. The instrument of choice is almost always the *human* instrument, which, while perhaps not quite so reliable or focused in the traditional

sense, is infinitely adaptable, capable of changing purpose and mode as the design becomes clearer. Even those considerations that appear to be included in both naturalistic and positivistic research protocols have very different meaning. In positivism, for example, data analysis procedures are usually determined before data collection methods are considered (that is precisely what statisticians mean when they speak of "experimental design"). In naturalistic inquiry, data collection and data analyses go on in concurrent and integrated steps that build on one another, with the first modicum of data collected yielding an initial analysis that in turn leads to additional, more focused data collection, which leads to a second data analysis effort, and so on and on, in hermeneutic-dialectic fashion. In this book, these processes are discussed separately only as a pedagogic convenience, not as a rational necessity. In some cases the naturalistic study substitutes a parallel form for that existing in positivism; thus, the naturalistic inquiry report takes the form of a case study rather than of the traditional technical (often statistical) paper or book, as described in Chapter 8.

8. *Naturalistic findings are created, not discovered.* The reader must be aware that the findings of naturalistic inquiry are not "discovered," that usage is also a remnant of positivist thinking. Naturalistic findings are, rather, literally *created* through the hermeneutic-dialectic interaction between and among the inquirer and various implicated groups (I prefer to think of them as stakeholders) found in the setting being investigated. The interaction leads to destruction and reconstruction all around; the hope is that consensus may be achieved on some emergent construction that provides stimulus and guidance for action (although that hope may well not be realized). In this process the formal inquirer is but the *primus inter pares*, a first among equals. Creation of the emergent construction is a joint effort. That construction can be successful, both in terms of the commitment it fosters and the action it stimulates, only to the extent that it is shared, "bought into," by most stakeholders. This point should be clear after a reading of Chapter 6.

So much for "stumbling blocks." Let me say again that these problems are not unique to this book and would hold equally true for any book that deals with alternative paradigm inquiry in any depth. But, of course, this collection of caveats is hardly what this book is about; it is in the main about *practice*. And this aspect is handled exceedingly well. Most contingencies that one can imagine arising in a naturalistic inquiry are dealt with. Beginning near the middle of Chapter 2, process aspects are the chief concern; the reader is walked through the entire process from problem identification to the final report. Each discussion is augmented and buttressed with a variety of real examples.

Perhaps the best feature of this practical book is the provision of exercises, which are thought-provoking and challenging. They display sequence and continuity from chapter to chapter. Some of the exercises also provide the opportunity to practice that most esoteric of the naturalist's skills—the hermeneutic-dialectic. A continuing exercise over all chapters is the conceptualization and development of a naturalistic study that the student might actually undertake (and portions of which he or she does undertake as part of the exercises). What students do with these exercises undoubtedly will also furnish a basis for many classroom questions and discussions. If learning by doing is a meaningful concept, students using this book as a classroom text will surely learn a great deal.

In summary, this book is as good a practical guide to naturalistic inquiry as one could hope for at this time. It is clear, it is practical, it is stimulating; it leads, it guides, it inspires. The authors provide action-based legitimation for naturalistic inquiry. If the question "It all sounds good, but does it work?" is a reasonable one to pose, then this book demonstrates that naturalistic inquiry works. But it is clear that the authors are *sharing*, not *imposing*, methods—or even recommending them. The reader is assumed to interact with the material; the methods presented cannot simply be generalized into other settings but must be assessed vicariously as personal experience might be assessed: to see if it fits and works in any new setting into which transfer might be proposed.

I have no doubt that this book will appeal to a variety of audiences, some of whom will be well versed in the theories of alternative paradigms, while others will be experiencing their first brush with these ideas. The former group may find some parts of the book repetitive and tedious, while the latter may find those same parts insufficient to enable a meaningful grasp of essentials. To the former group I would say that what seem to be redundancies can well be skipped over; the latter group will no doubt find it useful to consult other, more basic works, of which many are listed in the references. But I believe that both groups will find the principles guiding the *doing* of naturalistic inquiry useful and the examples thereof illuminating.

The authors are to be congratulated for a splendid contribution.

Egon G. Guba
College Station, Texas

Preface

THIS VOLUME SEEKS to take the reader on an adventure in research. At the same time, however, we recognize that not every reader will see such an adventure in this book. For the individual who has experience in conducting ethnographic or other qualitative studies, the volume perhaps may appear to have nothing more to offer than a somewhat different way of looking at a context to be studied. We encourage such readers to try hard to integrate the point of view that shared constructions, developed collaboratively by empowered individuals, are the basis for significant cross-cultural and interpersonal understandings. There will also be some readers who, being thoroughly trained in a prevailing methodology that focuses on the identification of variables, the formation of null hypotheses, and the statistical representation of magnitudes and relationships, may conclude early that the type of research promoted in this volume (and its not too subtle attacks on the prevailing methodology) is not only irreverent but irrelevant as well. We would like to urge these individuals to go through the entire book, complete the exercises, and try to withhold judgment until they have had a chance to test the power of naturalistic inquiry. There will also be those who, like the writers, have been frustrated by the limitations of prevailing methodology. For these individuals there is particular opportunity for an adventure in research, and we hope they find in this book a way of collecting, analyzing, and reporting data that frees them to answer previously unanswerable questions in a trustworthy fashion. Then there will be individuals who are brand new to the field of research, and we hope that they become hooked on the business of formulating, following, and developing answers to significant questions about social contexts in a manner that empowers not only the researcher but also every individual in these contexts.

The Limitations of This Book

The mode of research followed in this book has certain similarities with other types of research that are sometimes lumped together as "qualitative research." Many of the methods recommended in this book are very much like those that have been proposed and developed more extensively by other authors. Because we consider it beyond the scope of this text to provide a detailed description of the range of methods that are available, we will recommend some of these other authors to our readers and will occasionally refer to them throughout the text. In particular, we would recommend the works of Bogdan (Bogdan, 1972; Bogdan & Biklen, 1982; Bogdan & Taylor, 1975), Habenstein (1970), and Miles and Huberman (1984). What distinguishes this practical book from other texts on qualitative methods and procedures is not the particular methods that are presented, but the use of these methods to elicit and share human constructions of reality in social contexts. However, it is not our purpose to comprehensively provide the philosophical rationale for what we propose. As will become clearer in the first chapter, we feel that Egon Guba and Yvonna Lincoln (Guba, 1978; Guba, 1981; Guba & Lincoln, 1981; Guba & Lincoln, 1989; Lincoln, 1989; Lincoln & Guba, 1985) have done this job for us. Rather, it is our purpose to outline and bring the prospective researcher through a process that unites the underlying research philosophy on the one hand with specific methodology on the other in a production of a piece of research that meets standards of quality and is addressed to significant questions.

Using the Book

We think this book is best considered as a unified approach to research. We have confidence, based on experience, that the sequence of procedures outlined here can enhance the new researcher's ability to produce a significant piece of trustworthy research. For this reason we do not consider most of the "For Further Study" items at the end of each chapter to be optional; each is designed to provide practical learning in some critical area. The only exceptions are the third "For Further Study" items in the first and final chapters. The optional item in the first chapter is designed for those students who seek a clearer conceptual understanding before proceeding. The optional item in the final chapter opens the possibility for actually implementing the study that has been planned while going through the book. Furthermore, because these items build on each other from chapter to chapter, the products from each chapter should be retained so that they can be extended in subsequent chapters. In organizing the book in this way we do not intend to substitute our judgment for that of a course instructor, who, being closer to the students, may well construct alternative exercises. However, we do feel that students should receive guided practice in each area suggested by these items. We believe that the amount of work required to appropriately respond to these items is consistent with what can normally be expected in a graduate course of instruction.

In particular, the "For Further Study" items will recommend that the researcher become acquainted with several extended studies. We think it is important that the emerging researcher have the opportunity to review a range of exemplary research done in social contexts. These particular extended studies, however, are only suggestions. There are many other excellent studies; we encourage the reader to identify them and use them, either in lieu of or in addition to those we have suggested. Research done in social contexts usually makes for enjoyable reading, and we believe that the value of reading complete studies cannot be overestimated.

We also realize that not all students who embark on this adventure will have the same background. We believe, however, that any graduate student intent on improving his or her research skills can benefit from it. Many of the examples we provide have been taken from successful doctoral dissertation studies; we believe that these will be particularly helpful to graduate students who still have that experience ahead of them. Students who have extensive background in research methodology should get into the work easily. We encourage those with more limited backgrounds to be patient and to keep working to improve their skills. We will be developing an approach to research that is validated not so much by conformity to a set of rules and procedures as by the requirement for providing useful insight and direction for the context on which the research focuses. It is an open process that we propose, and we encourage the student to be open to growth in it.

Contents of the Book

The first two chapters set the foundation for the remainder of the book by considering the contribution of naturalistic inquiry and examining its assumptions and requirements. Chapter 1 presents a posture toward research that we believe should be evident in every researcher, but which is particularly critical for the scholar who would "do" naturalistic inquiry in social contexts. We examine some of the problems that confront researchers who study human activity in social settings and propose that many of these problems are the direct result of a conventional methodology that establishes artificial standards for rigor at the expense of relevance for practical decisions. Some alternative approaches to finding meaning in social situations are explored, and we consider briefly how underlying paradigms and assumptions about the world affect how one will conduct research and what can be expected from it. The naturalistic paradigm is proposed as a suitable base for conducting research in social contexts. Chapter 2 considers how individuals construct and communicate reality. It then examines the basic criteria for trustworthiness that underlie all research and briefly describes how the naturalistic paradigm proposes to meet these criteria. The implications of the paradigm for selection of methods and for data collection and analysis are also briefly examined.

Chapters 3 and 4 are designed to guide the new researcher in the initial stages of a naturalistic study. Chapter 3 deals with the processes by which a researcher gets started on a naturalistic study. We examine how a research problem is identified, how research questions are formulated, and how working hypotheses evolve to guide the researchers. We also explore the problems of identifying a suitable site for the research and gaining access to it. Chapter 4 looks at how a naturalistic study is designed. Because naturalistic inquiry rejects the artificial constraints that conventional methodology places on research, including that of an a priori design, the whole question of what is meant by "designing" a study must be reconsidered. Guidelines for nurturing an "emergent design" are given, and some direction for the early stages of the study is provided.

The fifth and sixth chapters examine the interactive processes of data collection and analysis. The collection of data is the topic of Chapter 5. Practical direction is given for gathering data from interviews, observations, documents, and artifacts. Chapter 6 looks at data analysis as it interacts with data as they are being collected as well as after they have been collected. The use of negative cases, data-based debates, and triangulated hypothesis testing as tools for analysis are proposed.

Important final considerations for the conduct of a naturalistic study are considered in Chapters 7 and 8. Chapter 7 examines the criteria by which the quality of a naturalistic study may be judged. It expands on the direction that had been given in Chapter 2 for establishing trustworthiness and describes procedures for ensuring that trustworthiness is built into the study. Chapter 7 also defines authenticity criteria for a naturalistic study and describes how they are satisfied. In addition, ethical considerations in a naturalistic study are discussed. Chapter 8 considers how the report of the study should be prepared in order to communicate effectively to the intended audience(s) and to support the overall purposes of the inquiry.

The Afterword reflects on the process of doing naturalistic inquiry, including some of the personal costs that are associated with it. It concludes with some final direction and encouragement for getting started on what is likely to be an exciting intellectual and practical adventure.

Acknowledgments

We would like to thank Yvonna Lincoln for her encouragement to write this text and her wisdom and guidance as we pursued it. A very special note of thanks is due to Sau-King (Joann) Young, who retyped several drafts of the text, worked many hours to integrate the efforts of four authors who were physically separated by hundreds of miles, and lent her own special expertise to preparing the final manuscript.

1

A Posture Toward Research:
The Need for a New Paradigm

WE HAVE WRITTEN this book at least partially because we have seen the wonder go out of research for many researchers, and we would like to help restore it. Many researchers seem to treat their work as a routine exercise, following very specific rules and denying much of the human capacity for flexible thinking, the extension of which, we believe, is the basis for scientific advance and the most satisfying aspect of research. Though we will follow a research paradigm that runs counter to the prevailing one, we nevertheless really believe that "good research is good research" and that whatever model significant research follows, it will capitalize on the wonderful flexible capacity of the human mind. Our posture toward research is caught fairly well by the following story, from more than a century ago, about research training in a field very different from our own.

LOOK AT YOUR FISH[1]

Samuel H. Scudder

Every Saturday, April 4, 1874.

It was more than fifteen years ago that I entered the laboratory of Professor Agassiz, and told him I had enrolled my name in the Scientific School as a student of natural history. He asked me a few questions about my object in coming, my antecedents generally, the mode in which I afterwards proposed to use the knowledge I might acquire, and, finally, whether I wished to study any special branch. To the latter I replied that, while I wished to be well grounded in all departments of zoology, I purposed to devote myself specially to insects.

"When do you wish to begin?" he asked.

"Now," I replied.

This seemed to please him, and with an energetic "Very Well!" he reached from a shelf a huge jar of specimens in yellow alcohol. "Take this fish," he said, "and look at it; we call it a haemulon; by and by I will ask what you have seen."

With that he left me, but in a moment returned with explicit instructions as to the care of the object entrusted to me.

"No man is fit to be a naturalist," said he, "who does not know how to take care of specimens."

I was to keep the fish before me in a tin tray, and occasionally moisten the surface with alcohol from the jar, always taking care to replace the stopper tightly. Those were not the days of ground-glass stoppers and elegantly shaped exhibition jars; all the old students will recall the huge neckless glass bottles with their leaky, wax-besmeared corks, half eaten by insects, and begrimed with cellar dust. Entomology was a cleaner science than ichthyology, but the example of the Professor, who had unhesitatingly plunged to the bottom of the jar to produce the fish, was infectious; and though this alcohol had a "very ancient and fishlike smell," I really dared not show any aversion within these sacred precincts, and treated the alcohol as though it were pure water. Still I was conscious of a passing feeling of disappointment, for gazing at a fish did not commend itself to an ardent entomologist. My friends, at home, too, were annoyed when they discovered that no amount of eau-de-Cologne would drown the perfume which haunted me like a shadow.

In ten minutes I had seen all that could be seen in that fish, and started in search of the Professor—who had, however, left the Museum; and when I returned, after lingering over some of the odd animals stored in the upper apartment, my specimen was dry all over. I dashed the fluid over the fish as if to resuscitate the beast from a fainting fit, and looked with anxiety for a return of the normal sloppy appearance. This little excitement over, nothing was to be done but to return to a steadfast gaze at my mute companion. Half an hour passed—an hour—another hour; the fish began to look loathsome. I turned it over and around; looked it in the face—ghastly; from behind, beneath, above, sideways, at a three-quarters' view—just as ghastly. I was in despair; at an early hour I concluded that lunch was necessary; so, with infinite relief, the fish was carefully replaced in the jar, and for an hour I was free.

On my return, I learned that Professor Agassiz had been at the Museum, but had gone, and would not return for several hours. My fellow-students were too busy to be disturbed by continued conversation. Slowly I drew forth that hideous fish, and with a feeling of desperation again looked at it. I might not use a magnifying-glass; instruments of all kinds were interdicted. My two hands, my two eyes, and the fish; it seemed a most limited field. I pushed my finger down its throat to feel how sharp the teeth were. I began to count the scales in the different rows, until I was convinced that that was nonsense. At last a happy thought struck me—I would draw the fish; and now with surprise I began to discover new features in the creature. Just then the Professor returned.

"That is right," said he; " a pencil is one of the best of eyes. I am glad to notice, too, that you keep your specimen wet, and your bottle corked."

With these encouraging words, he added:

"Well, what is it like?"

He listened attentively to my brief rehearsal of the structure of parts who names were still unknown to me: the fringed gill-arches and moveable operculum; the pores of the head, fleshy lips and lidless eyes; the lateral line, the spinous fins and forked tail; the compressed and arched body. When I finished, he waited as if expecting more, and then, with an air of disappointment:

"You have not looked very carefully; why," he continued more earnestly, "you haven't even seen one of the most conspicuous features of the animal, which is as plainly before your eyes as the fish itself; look again, look again!" and he left me to my misery.

I was piqued; I was mortified. Still more of that wretched fish! But now I set myself to my task with a will, and discovered one new thing after another, until I saw how just the Professor's criticism had been. The afternoon passed quickly; and when, towards its close, the Professor inquired:

"Do you see it yet?"

"No," I replied, "I am certain I do not, but I see how little I saw before."

"That is next best," said he, earnestly, "But I won't hear you now; put away your fish and go home; perhaps you will be ready with a better answer in the morning. I will examine you before you look at the fish."

This was disconcerting. Not only must I think of my fish all night, studying, without the object before me, what this unknown but most visible feature might be; but also, without reviewing my discoveries, I must give an exact account of them the next day. I had a bad memory; so I walked home by Charles River in a distracted state with my two perplexities.

The cordial greeting from the Professor the next morning was reassuring; here was a man who seemed to be quite as anxious as I that I should see for myself what he saw.

"Do you perhaps mean," I asked, "that the fish has symmetrical sides with paired organs?"

His thoroughly pleased "Of course! of course!" repaid the wakeful hours of the previous night. After he had discoursed most happily and enthusiastically—as he always did—upon the importance of this point, I ventured to ask what I should do next.

"Oh, look at your fish!" he said, and left me again to my own devices. In a little more than an hour he returned, and heard my new catalogue.

"That is good, that is good!" he repeated; "but that is not all; go on"; and so for three long days he placed that fish before my eyes, forbidding me to look at anything else, or to use any artificial aid. "Look, look, look," was his repeated injunction.

This was the best entomological lesson I ever had—a lesson whose influence has extended to the details of every subsequent study; a legacy the Professor had left to me, as he has left it to so many others, of inestimable value, which we could not buy, with which we cannot part.

We would urge anyone who aspires to meaningful research to take a stance similar to that mandated by Professor Agassiz (though we will find that the task of the naturalistic researcher, who interacts with the languages and meanings of human beings, is much more complex than examining a soggy fish). This stance is particularly important for doctoral students, for whom the dissertation is likely to be the first significant piece of independent research in which they will be involved. For a certain proportion of these students the dissertation will be the first step in research careers; the habits and attitudes they develop in their dissertation studies are likely to be those that characterize what they do subsequently. Much of the research that is used to provide examples in this book is doctoral dissertation research and may be particularly relevant to those who are at this stage in their careers.

The pedagogical posture taken by Professor Agassiz is also instructive for our purposes. He did not prescribe a set of rules and procedures for his student to follow, only the admonition: "Look at your fish!" Yet not all of the student's observations were of equal worth. Observations were validated by the sloppy, lifeless form of a fish placed in front of the student and by logical extensions from those observations. This is very similar to the process that we will try to develop in this book. The process of observing, recording, analyzing, reflecting, dialoguing, and rethinking are all essential parts of the research process as we seek to develop it. All are validated by their contributions to understanding the context in which the observed events have taken place. The importance of context will be examined further later in this chapter.

Research in Social Settings

In this initial chapter of the text we note briefly some of the frustrations that good researchers of human interaction have experienced in doing their work. These frustrations, it appears, have not come entirely from the complexities of the fields they have been researching but from a prevailing model for research that has denied access to some potentially powerful research tools and procedures. This chapter explores some alternative procedures that have been tried and briefly describes current thinking about a shift in research paradigms. It concludes with a brief consideration of the critical importance of social context in doing naturalistic inquiry.

In an article in *The Sport Psychologist*, Rainer Martens (1987) recounted his own experience as a researcher:

> For about 15 years I studied sport psychology using the methods of science that had been taught to me in graduate school. As the years passed I became increasingly discontent with these methods, not because of lack of interest in the phenomena I was studying, for I am today even more fascinated with the subject matter of sport psychology. Instead, I became dissatisfied with the methods for studying the phenomena of our field, but I did not fully understand why. I could not explain it intellectually, but emotionally these methods did not "seem right" for wanting to truly understand human behavior (p. 29).

With minor adjustments Martens's statement would probably describe the experience of many researchers whose major focus has been on human behavior and the settings in which that behavior takes place. Students of educational organizations have regularly been disappointed in how feeble the "best" research methods have been in obtaining answers to significant questions. If what Martens senses is accurate and if it reflects a general dilemma for students of human behavior, then what it suggests is that what have been considered the "best methods" are not good enough.

In an article in *Social Service Review* (1981), Heineman noted the impact of methodology and design in the field of social work:

[T]he prevailing model of social work research posits a hierarchy of research designs [that] runs the gamut from least to most scientific and is ordered by the extent to which the criterion of prediction and its concomitant requirements—such as experimental manipulation, control groups, and randomization—are satisfied. (p. 374)

She goes on to say:

The problem is not that these assumptions about what constitutes good science and hence good social work research never lead to useful knowledge, but, rather, that they are used normatively, rather than descriptively, to prescribe some research methodologies and proscribe others. (p. 374)

Heineman contends that the prescriptive nature of current social work conceptualizations of science, as embodied in the preferred forms of research design and methodology, effectively determine the nature of practice rather than allowing practice to determine the form of scientific inquiry.

The experience of Martens and the comments of Heineman ring true for the authors of this book, and we suspect they do also for many readers. We have easily accepted the prescriptions of the scientific method without questioning its underlying assumptions, particularly the assumption of the objectivity of knowledge. Since our days in elementary school we have heard the virtues of the scientific method extolled and have thoroughly digested the history that was presented to us of its contributions to human welfare. The ingrained bias in favor of an oversimplified representation of the scientific method has often led us to question ourselves and our abilities when the results we have achieved have been unresponsive to the problems we have posed. We have persistently hoped for statistical procedures and computer capabilities that would enable us to quantify and manipulate the subtle and complex differences that we encounter in social settings, never suspecting that objective quantification might be a part of the problem, not the solution.

Martens found himself living two different lives:

I have come to know quite intimately two very different sport psychologies—what I term *academic sport psychology* and *practicing sport psychology*. They have caused me to lead two very different lives. One is academic, scientific, and abstract; the other practical, applied and, as seen by some, mystical. Why are these two sport psychologies on diverging courses? The answer, I contend, lies in sport psychologists' perceptions of what constitutes legitimate knowledge. (p. 30)

According to Martens, the chief concern of academic sport psychology is the application of the rules of science in a way that is considered acceptable by behavioral researchers. However, he found that his second life as a practicing sport psychologist was considerably more productive because he gained more knowledge by practicing sport psychology than he did from using the orthodox scientific method to study sport psychology. Martens sees this disjuncture between the two methods of identifying and acquiring "legitimate knowledge" as reflective of what Thomas Kuhn (1970) associates with a paradigm crisis.

A paradigm, according to Kuhn, provides a way of looking at the world. It exerts influence on a field of study by providing the assumptions, the rules, the direction, and the criteria by which "normal science" is carried out. The accepted work of scientists in a field of study consists of working out the details that are implied by the paradigm and, in so doing, fulfilling the promise of the paradigm. But as Kuhn demonstrates in a number of different fields, this work inevitably produces anomalies that cannot be fully contained by the prevailing paradigm. This paves the way for a new paradigm (for example, the replacement of a geocentric view of the universe with a heliocentric view) that better explains the anomalies and enables a new phase of normal science to be initiated. However, the shift from an old paradigm to a new one is typically not smooth. The older, established scientists within a field have built their careers around the earlier paradigm, and they control the rules by which rewards are given for scientific work. The conflict continues until the emergent paradigm prevails, usually not until the older paradigm has died, along with the last of the eminent scientists who protected it.

Haworth, writing in *Social Service Review* (1984), considers the implications of the Kuhnian theses for the social sciences:

> Whether one agrees with all the implications of Kuhn's historical analysis, one consequence is observable. Since 1962, an increasing "consciousness of paradigm" has been chipping away at the assumptions of social scientists. The pressure has been toward making the intuitive and implicit more explicit. . . . This process is even more chaotic in the preparadigmatic social sciences, where assumptions are generally borrowed naively, learned authoritatively, and held tenaciously. (p. 351)

Probably the broadest statement regarding a shift in paradigms has been provided by Peter Schwartz and James Ogilvy in their monograph, *The Emergent Paradigm: Changing Patterns of Thought and Belief* (1979).

From their analysis of what is happening in a wide variety of fields of study, including physics, linguistics, and the arts, they concluded that a new general paradigm is emerging that challenges the assumptions and beliefs of the "scientific method" that currently dominates scholarly research. The pursuit of the new paradigm has been most comprehensively applied to knowledge generation and research in the field of education by Egon Guba and Yvonna Lincoln (Guba, 1978; Guba, 1981; Guba & Lincoln, 1981; Guba & Lincoln, 1989; Lincoln, 1989; Lincoln & Guba, 1985). This new paradigm was originally explicated by Guba and Lincoln as the "naturalistic" paradigm (Guba, 1981; Guba & Lincoln, 1981; Lincoln & Guba, 1985), though in recent years they have preferred the term "constructivist" to "naturalistic" because of several implications of the latter term (Guba & Lincoln, 1989). However, in this book we will continue to use the term *naturalistic* when referring to the new paradigm and the mode of inquiry associated with it.

It would be hard to overestimate the contribution that the writings and presentations of Guba and Lincoln have made to this present volume. Their work has carefully examined the assumptions and difficulties of the prevailing paradigm, systematically explicated and extended the philosophical foundations and procedural implications of the new paradigm, provided an initial codification of the safeguards to inquiry under the new paradigm, and taken on the major battles and debates that have arisen from the paradigm crisis. While we are less certain than Lincoln and Guba about the precise nature of the new paradigm, we do agree with Lincoln (1989) that the debate involves a "whole paradigm" shift and cannot be resolved by tinkering with methods or with isolated axioms of scientific inquiry.

We do not, however, wish in the text to become directly involved in what Nathaniel Gage has labeled the "paradigm wars" (Gage, 1989). This debate has focused on the suitability of various alternatives to what proponents of a new paradigm have labeled "positivism" (Eisner, 1992; Erickson, 1992; Popkewitz, 1992; Schrag, 1992). Our reading of the literature suggests that the term *positivism* has become very muddled because of its alternative uses in either its original philosophical sense or an extended meaning to cover nearly all the conventions surrounding mainstream research procedures, a term that some have used as a claim to nearly everything that is good in research, others have used to include nearly everything that is bad, and still others have dismissed as an irrelevant term. As we follow the debate, we are convinced that the two sides often use this term to talk past each other. For this reason, we generally avoid the term *positivism* in this text.

Nor do we take space in this book to examine alternative manifestations of a new paradigm, such as those explicated in the educational connoisseurship of Eisner (1985) or the critical theory of Popkewitz (1984). Instead, as we have noted, in the text we attempt to take the naturalistic-constructivist model developed by Egon Guba and Yvonna Lincoln and give practical guidance, built on experience, for using it to do research. We will not attack positivism per se, but we do know, as Martens discussed, that traditional research conventions that are taught in our major universities have kept researchers of human behavior from systematically asking and obtaining practical answers to important questions. Lincoln and Guba's naturalistic inquiry and constructivism is probably not the only suitable alternative to current conventions, but we know from experience that it offers a workable rationale for performing significant research in human settings. This volume attempts to communicate the craft knowledge that has been acquired from a series of serious attempts to apply the alternative assumptions and procedures of the naturalistic paradigm to inquiry in education. It is intended to provide a transferable base for others who would like to pursue important questions in educational organizations but have been regularly baffled by the rigors and assumptions of the prevailing paradigm.

The Quest for Relevance: Some Different Approaches

Some years ago (before the naturalistic paradigm had been articulated) one of the authors was a member of a team of consultants that took on the task of evaluating the educational program of a large state institution. The team's charge was no more specific than this. Within the team the author's particular task was to conduct an overall organizational analysis of the institution. Other team members looked at clinical procedures, curriculum, testing, and instructional practices. Because their charge had been nebulous, the team members took the approach that they would need to look at a broad range of data to "see what was happening" and to help them understand the organization. Team members examined records, interviewed individuals at all levels of the institution, and spent considerable time observing classes and interpersonal interactions throughout the organization. Though the five team members worked independently and kept their own schedules, they did come together at several points to compare notes and make subsequent plans for the conduct of the study.

Almost surprisingly, their different investigations led to major convergent conclusions:

1. Educational activities were energetically and enthusiastically performed by competent people with high morale.
2. Conceptions of the educational mission were fragmented and differed considerably among the various subsystems of the institution.
3. As a result, even though communication within the organization was pervasive, well-intentioned activity by various individuals and groups often led to overall dysfunctional results.

These conclusions, though simple, were dynamic and enabled the institution to see itself in a different light. On the basis of their evaluation the team members made a number of recommendations for action that enabled the institution to enhance its performance. However, what will be considered here are some observations that might be drawn from the brief description of how this evaluation study proceeded:

1. *The nebulous charge to the consultation team considered as an asset.* At the time the charge was given, most of the team members (accustomed to operating with traditional evaluation models) wished that it were more specific. However, a more typical, specific charge would doubtless have screened out much of the information that was found. In fact, with the benefit of hindsight, it is hard to imagine the evaluation objectives that might have been stated or the battery of tests and instruments that might have been prescribed in advance, without the knowledge that was obtained from this study, that would lead to similar fertile results. The simple question "What's happening here?" (worded in many different ways) provided a tremendous amount of rich data that team members were able to interpret in light of their own extensive backgrounds as researchers.

2. *Convergent conclusions from divergent data.* The team members came to very similar conclusions from looking at very dissimilar data sets. However, while they all looked at different aspects of the institution and its operations, they were all guided by the same holistic question: "What's happening here?" Had they asked specific, discrete questions guided by their separate areas of expertise, they would have come up with specific indices that would not naturally converge to produce a comprehensive, meaningful picture or a basis for action. Achievement and ability scores, organizational climate indices, and instructional objectives (all of which provide specific, quantified data on key aspects of the problem) would,

in this case at least, have provided specific results that suggested divergent and conflicting sources of the problem and interpretations of the problem itself. In fact, for even one of these dimensions (e.g., organizational climate), standard instruments would have provided a mixed bag of results with significant alternative interpretations.

What is at issue here is a very different view of reality from that held by the prevailing traditions of behavioral science. The prevailing scientific paradigm assumes that there is a single objective reality, ascertainable through the five senses and their extensions (e.g., microscopes, telescopes, sonograms, etc.). This objective reality can be divided into successively smaller particles (e.g., molecules, atoms, electrons) that are governed by a common set of "laws." Because the "building blocks" of reality are the same across time and space and are governed by universal scientific laws, we can (in theory at least) logically assemble and disassemble them, aggregate and disaggregate them, and, by observing results, make conclusions that can be generalized to other situations with the same conditions and building blocks. Furthermore, because all bits of reality are pieces of a total Reality, the results obtained from one well-done study will add logically to the results found from other studies. When results lead to incongruous meanings, it can be explained only by inadequate instrumentation, inadequate application of the instrumentation, or a study that was not adequately controlled. Good researchers, particularly in the social sciences, work overtime to find more precise instruments, more powerful statistical procedures to manipulate the data obtained through their instruments, or at least a more "typical" setting (preferably a large number of typical settings to overcome random error) in which their instruments can be applied.

The new paradigm proposes a reality that is of "whole cloth." That is, all aspects of reality are interrelated. To isolate one aspect from its context destroys much of its meaning. Guba (1981) notes that "if one attempts to focus attention on certain portions of reality only, the whole falls apart as though the cloth had been cut with a scissors" (pp. 77-78). On the other hand, by looking holistically at even a corner of the cloth or at a piece taken from the middle of it, we can usually predict with great accuracy the nature of the entire piece of cloth. This is why the team members in the study described here (whether clinician, special educator, early childhood educator, or organizational analyst) came up with such convergent conclusions from looking at such divergent data.

However, the new paradigm also assumes that there is not a single objective reality but multiple realities of which the researcher must be aware. Extended research leads to a rich awareness of divergent realities rather than to convergence on a single reality. The researchers in this study found that different realities had been constructed by the various groups and individuals in the organization and formed the boundaries of their understanding of the organization and provided the framework for the way they would behave in it. Their own convergent conclusions represented a new constructed reality, based on these divergent realities and negotiated among themselves, that added to the meaning of the realities constructed by the various individuals and groups in the organization. Communication of this newly constructed reality to persons in the organization, and construction of a new, richer reality, would provide the basis for relevant action by the organization.

3. *No cause and effect; mutual simultaneous shaping.* The observations of the team showed some comprehensive patterns and relationships but certainly showed no cause and effect. Why was there high morale while at the same time there was a fragmented understanding of the organization's mission? Why did pervasive communication not provide common understandings? Would less communication have provided better understanding? Would a clear understanding of the organization's mission have resulted in lower morale? It was clear to the consultation team that such questions were naive and simplistic. So, however, were any other suggestions that a simple cause of the organization's malaise could be identified and, by implication, that a simple straightforward remedy could be applied. All the factors observed were bound together in a whole cloth pattern in which each part was dependent on every other part. Each part was both cause and effect of every other part, a situation described by Lincoln and Guba (1985) as "mutual simultaneous shaping." Any solution to the problem would have to be a holistic one that addressed the overall pattern of the organization's behavior and not just some portion of it.

4. *Nongeneralizable results; no preordinate design; no scholarly publications.* In many ways this was a very atypical organization. There may not be another half dozen like it in the nation that could be included with it in a common study of the characteristics examined in this evaluation effort. Furthermore, there were no controls imposed on the collection or analysis of data, no preordinate design (unless a design is constituted by a team of evaluators from different backgrounds agreeing in advance about what general areas they will observe), no pre- and posttests, no randomization. Design for the study emerged in the process of the team's observations; theory did not govern the collection of data but was used on occasion after data had been analyzed to better communicate what had been observed.

All of this is guaranteed to make the traditionally trained researcher very nervous.

Furthermore, the study would not generally be considered a scholarly endeavor. It could be generalized to no other setting; there were no others exactly like this one. And the team members interacted far too much with the setting and the people in it to retain their objectivity. What was learned that would be transferable to another setting was something about the general procedures that govern a study such as this one. Also, a thick description of the operations of this institution would provide the basis for allowing readers to determine if this study could provide insights for their own. Many scholarly journals would not be disposed to publish such a study, no matter how much was learned or no matter how great the impact on the institution for which it was done.

The very atypical nature of this study makes it an excellent one to illustrate some of the major differences between the prevailing and emerging paradigms. While this institution was indeed an extreme case that provided for no generalizability, it highlighted a central truth: No two social settings are sufficiently similar to allow simplistic, sweeping generalizations from one to another. No two atoms are identical. How much more disparate are any two social settings, regardless of surface similarities, when they are made up of different, complex individuals related in multitudinous undefined ways? Traditional research methods attempt to solve this problem by trying to focus only on categorized variables that appear across settings; the categorization masks the differences; undefined interrelationships of these categorized variables with the environment are "controlled" through randomization. (All hydrogen atoms can be classified together; all chairs can be classified together; all 3-year-old boys can be classified together; all science laboratories can be classified together.) Many proponents of a new paradigm, including Lincoln and Guba, attempt to solve the problem by not attempting to generalize. But researchers who do generalize are more likely to have their writings published in scholarly journals. Yet, significant answers to context-unique complex questions cannot be generalized across different human settings. This was the difficulty noted by Martens as he found himself torn between academic sport psychology and practicing sport psychology. It was the latter that provided information to significant questions. Real problems always appear in particular contexts and, while relevant data leading to resolution may come from many sources, their solutions are always bound by those contexts.

Paradigms, Assumptions, and Implications for Research

As this brief case review has indicated, the prevailing and emergent paradigms make very different assumptions about reality, objectivity, and generalization. These different assumptions have important implications for the way research is conducted. In this section we shall review the different assumptions of the two paradigms and consider briefly their implications.

As noted earlier the prevailing paradigm assumes that there is a single objective reality that is ascertainable through the five senses, subject to universal laws of science, and manipulable through the logical processes of the mind. From this basic assumption several corollaries follow. First, knowledge accumulation is incremental. When a person encounters new information it is assessed to determine how it fits with previous knowledge and theory. Dissonance with previous knowledge either means that the present data are flawed, previous data are flawed, or the theory linking them is flawed. Generally, a case against the new data is assumed until an overwhelming case can be made against either existing knowledge or theory. A second corollary that flows from this first one is that the process for accumulating knowledge is self-correcting. Logical error, random error, and inadequate data are problems to be overcome through improved logic, increased sample size, or further research. Differences of perception can be resolved through filling the gaps in individuals' knowledge and correcting the flaws in their logic.

The naturalistic paradigm assumes, however, that there are multiple realities, with differences among them that cannot be resolved through rational processes or increased data. In fact, extended inquiry along a priori paths will result in a greater divergence of data; convergence comes only as the interrelationships between all the elements of reality are seen. Because all the "parts" of reality are interrelated, an understanding of the "whole" can begin with a holistic investigation of any portion of it. By "understanding the whole" we refer to a working comprehension of the interrelationships that give definition to it. This is why the separate members of the consultation team came up with convergent conclusions by asking the same basic question ("What's happening here?") about the institution they were observing. However, while their conclusions converged, it is important to note that they were not isomorphic. There were indeed differences among them, as one would expect when different observers are looking at different data. But rather than trying to resolve these differences, these separate sets of observations were compared to observe what common meaning they could provide. Rather than providing a neat, sterile picture of congruent geometric figures, these separate observations provided a mosaic with general, unclear boundaries, but with rich central meanings about the interrelationships in the institution. The case for these rich central meanings was pervasive and provided the basis for relevant action. Multiple realities enhance each other's meanings; forcing them to a single precise definition emasculates meaning.

Objectivity is a goal of traditional research. Yet, as Lincoln and Guba (1985) have pointed out, it is largely an illusion. To try, through various safeguards, to maintain it while studying human interaction is an exercise that fails to fully safeguard the data from the researcher while inevitably serving as a barrier to prevent the researcher from exploring the most relevant aspects of the data. Rainer Martens (1987) noted it this way:

> It seems to me an enormous loss of knowledge that coaches and athletes with many years of experience are permitted to retire and never record, in some systematic way, their experiences. While the more famous may write their autobiographies, how much more could we learn if someone spent a month interviewing John Wooden, for example, to discover what he has learned about the psychology of sport? With your ability as a sport psychologist to ask probing questions, with your tacit knowledge to search for patterns, how much more would you learn by such an interview than by conducting another 2 × 2 factorial study in your laboratory? Most of us would delight in pursuing such knowledge because the yield would be so great. Yet at present we deny ourselves this approach because it does not fulfill the doctrine of objectivity, and thus is deemed unscientific. (pp. 50-51)

The naturalistic paradigm affirms the mutual influence that researcher and respondents have on each other. Nor are the dangers of reactivity ignored. However, never can formal methods be allowed to separate the researcher from the human interaction that is the heart of the research. To get to the relevant matters of human activity, the researcher must be involved in that activity. The dangers of bias and reactivity are great; the dangers of being insulated from relevant data are greater. The researcher must find ways to control the biases that do not inhibit the flow of pertinent information. Relevance cannot be sacrificed for the sake of rigor.

The prevailing view is that science grows through the accumulation of generalizable knowledge. However, as noted above, total generalization is never possible, even in the physical sciences. This principle of nongeneralizability is even more pertinent for study in the social sciences. Generalization across social settings depends on aggregation of data, a practice that often ignores the context-specific interrelationships that give those data meaning. Proponents of naturalistic inquiry, realizing the impossibility of generalizing, settle for a deep understanding and explication of social phenomena as they are observed in their own contexts. Transfer of understandings across social contexts depends on the degree to which thick description of one set of interrelationships in one social context allows for the formulation of "working hypotheses" (Guba, 1981) that can direct inquiry in another.

Guba (1981) examines the major implications for research that flow from the assumptions of the naturalistic paradigm. Most of these were evident in our brief review of the consultation team's activities and in our earlier discussion. We shall develop each of these throughout this volume. We present his list as a summary of the material presented in this chapter and as an introduction to later chapters.

1. While both qualitative and quantitative methods can be used, qualitative methods are generally preferred, primarily because they allow for thick data to be collected that demonstrate their interrelationship with their context.
2. While both relevance and rigor are important in research, relevance is paramount.
3. Grounded, emergent theory is preferred to a priori theory. All theory should be grounded at some stage before it is applied.
4. Tacit knowledge (including intuitions, apprehensions, or feelings) is treated differently but on an equal basis with propositional knowledge (knowledge that is explicated in language).
5. While the researcher may use a variety of instruments to gather data, the primary research instrument is the *researcher*.
6. Research design emanates from the research itself.
7. A natural setting is always preferred to a laboratory or controlled setting.

The Importance of Context in Naturalistic Inquiry

Naturalistic inquiry is very dependent upon context. This stems from its fundamental assumption that all the subjects of such an inquiry are bound together by a complex web of unique interrelationships that results in the mutual simultaneous shaping described earlier. This complex web of interrelationships provides a context that at one time both restricts and extends the applicability of the research. On the one hand, full generalizability to other settings becomes impossible because no two contexts are identical, and attempting to generalize about one phase of the context to other settings ignores the unique shaping forces that exist in each context. On the other hand, the intricacy of the context that is revealed by naturalistic inquiry permits applications to interpersonal settings that are impossible with most studies that follow prevailing research strategies.

While no naturalistic study ever describes or explains a context fully, a well-done naturalistic study can come closer to such an explanation than prevailing research strategies. Application is of two types: We can obtain direction for dealing with the same setting in the future or for further inquiry about similar settings. While not perfect, the best predictor of an organization's or community's behavior in the future is its behavior today. Similarly, a comprehensive understanding of Context A enables us to make useful judgments about similarities and differences in Context B.

As one of the authors has pointed out elsewhere (Erlandson, 1992), context provides great power for understanding and making predictions about social settings. He describes four experiences that particularly demonstrated the power of context to him. One of these has to do with the writing of a set of case studies. The case studies were built on data derived from the key human sources in various social settings and enriched with data from documents and records. As the case studies were developed, names were changed, locations were disguised, and other steps were taken to preserve the anonymity of the respondents. However, the basic relationships present in the social contexts were preserved. After the draft of a case study had been completed, the researcher asked each of the major respondents to read the case to see if it "rang true" in terms of faithfully describing the dynamics of what happened. Almost without exception, the major respondents, even those on opposite sides of a controversy, reported that the essence of the case had indeed been captured. What enabled this to happen was that the descriptive case study, by placing the respondents back in the context of their earlier experience, evoked the original emotions and judgments. Respondents on opposite sides of the controversy both believed that the case validated the positions they had taken.

Other experiences, reported in the same article, further substantiated the power of context for understanding human settings by enabling predictions about social contexts. One of these experiences related to the use of community power structure studies to predict future events for school districts. Detailed descriptions of social contexts enabled uncannily accurate predictions about future events. Another had to do with graduate students being able to correctly answer questions about school organizations other than their own (on items about which they had no specific data) by first reviewing data that described the social contexts of these organizations. Finally, this researcher was pleasantly surprised when, 10 years after he had conducted (but never formally reported) a naturalistic study of an organization, another naturalistic researcher, operating independently and without his knowledge, came to the same interpretations and confirmed that his predictions had been accurate.

Interpretation is both limited and enriched by context. Interpretation is limited as context drives constantly toward greater specificity; at the same time the accumulation of specific detail provided by context describes a set of intricate relationships that bring the researcher or reader vicariously into the setting. It is this exciting adventure in rich precision and diversity to which this book on "doing naturalistic inquiry" is dedicated.

For Further Study

1. Select two articles that use large quantitative data bases from recent issues of the *American Educational Research Journal*, the *Educational Administration Quarterly*, *Social Work Service*, or some other scholarly journal. After reading them, consider what you have learned from them and what might be done with the results. Then read two of the high school "portraits" from Sara L. Lightfoot's *The Good High School* (1983) and again consider what might be done with the results. Then compare your answers with others. What kinds of things do you learn from each type of study?

2. Begin laying plans for a naturalistic study that you will direct, conduct, or otherwise participate in as a research team member. At the present time use whatever knowledge and background you have to design this study. Primarily, begin by formulating two or three basic questions: for example, "What's happening here?" or "Why are things the way they are?" or "How do you make sense of things around here?" As you progress through this text, make modifications in this design based on the readings in the text, outside readings, and any additional background you may acquire.

3. For further clarification of the specific distinctions between the prevailing positivistic paradigm and emerging paradigms (including naturalistic-constructivist inquiry), you may wish to consult Chapter 1 of *The Paradigm Dialog* (Guba, 1990).

Note

1. *Look at Your Fish* was written by Samuel H. Scudder in 1874 and was extracted from McCrimmon (1968), pp. 74-77. Reprinted with premission © 1968, Houghton Mifflin Company.

2

≡

The Process of Inquiry:
Some Basic Considerations

IN CHAPTER 1 we included Samuel Scudder's account of how he learned to do research under Louis Agassiz because it so well illustrates the basic posture of humility that every researcher must assume in the face of how little he or she knows in comparison to how much there is to be known. By the end of his week with the fish, Scudder knew that he was just beginning to learn about the complexity of that lifeless object. Because our focus in this book will be on inquiring about human settings and interactions, which are many times more complex than Scudder's fish, we believe that the basic posture of humility and willingness to learn what was never imagined to be learnable when the researcher started is even more imperative.

Good researchers, representing every paradigmatic stance, are similarly awed by the depth and complexity of the fields they are investigating. However, for conventional researchers, the problem, while overwhelming, may still be approached in a relatively straightforward manner. For them reality is a single, consistent knowable piece that can be systematically divided into parts and subparts that can be apprehended through the five senses and their extensions (microscopes, telescopes, sonograms, etc.). Because these parts are discrete pieces of the whole, they can be reassembled when necessary. Knowledge can be incrementally accrued by examination of these parts. Every piece of new knowledge that is acquired is assigned its proper place in the taxonomies of previous knowledge and provides direction for the addition of other new increments of knowledge.

Such straightforward accumulation of knowledge is not possible for naturalistic researchers because they assume that human beings must operate within realities they themselves have constructed. Further, the constructed realities of no two human beings are identical. This means that researchers bring certain constructed realities to their research settings and in these human settings find other constructions of reality among their respondents.
 ⨏ When they attempt to communicate their findings to the research community or to the general public, they face similar difficulties. The process of inquiry for the naturalistic researcher becomes one of developing and verifying shared constructions that will enable the meaningful expansion of knowledge. This chapter will deal with the processes by which realities are constructed, communicated, and verified so that inquiry can be facilitated.

Constructing and Communicating Reality

The evidence of constructed realities is perhaps nowhere better seen than in the attempts of people with one primary language to communicate with people whose primary language is another. Only the naive observer who has never tried to communicate in-depth with people whose primary language is different would assume that the translation of one language into another is simply a matter of identifying all the equivalent words in both languages. Edward Sapir (Spier, 1941) and Benjamin Whorf (Whorf, 1956) made it clear years ago that language both shapes and is shaped by the experience of those who speak it as their primary tongue. Most persons in the United States get along quite well with one word for snow; according to Bryson (1990) the Eskimo uses more than 50 different words. We see snow. The Eskimo "sees" (i.e., comprehends and integrates) different things depending on which word is being used. The Aztecs, in a warmer climate, used the same word for "cold," "ice," and "snow." In the Hopi language, the equivalent of our nouns and verbs are distinguished by their duration; nouns denote longer duration and verbs denote shorter duration. Hence, "lightning," "flame," "meteor," "puff of smoke," and "wave" are verbs; "cloud" and "storm" barely make it over the duration threshold to be classified as nouns. Further, the Hopi language does not recognize time in the mathematical sense; nor does it have equivalent words for "velocity" or "matter." To a Westerner this seems to destroy the possibility of constructing a consistent picture of the universe. Yet the Hopi do have a consistent world view, one constructed according to a very different ideology and a very different experience (Whorf, 1956). It is important to note that one categorization scheme is no more "natural" than another one. It surely is difficult for most of us to understand the logic that drives the Hopi classification scheme, but this demonstrates the central point: The language we speak determines what we experience and in turn is driven by the categories we construct to make sense out of the world we experience.

An excellent picture of the relationship between language and the construction of reality is furnished by Helen Keller (1954) in the story of her life. Having become blind and deaf while still a small baby, Helen did not learn language until she was 7 years old and met Miss Sullivan. As Miss Sullivan tapped out words on her wrist, Helen discovered that two very different items (one a hard ceramic object and the other a soft cotton object) were both included in the word D-O-L-L. She found, with some difficulty, that W-A-T-E-R must be distinguished from the M-U-G in which it was contained. Words such as *love* took a little longer, but in learning them she constructed a reality that at once combined universal, cultural, and personal experiences into an understanding that was all her own. She noted:

> Everything had a name, and each name gave birth to a new thought. . . . I recall many incidents of the summer of 1887 that followed my soul's sudden awakening. I did nothing but explore with my hands and learn the name of every object that I touched; and the more I handled things and learned their names and uses, the more joyous and confident grew my sense of kinship with the rest of the world. (pp. 36-37)

Jean Piaget (1950) describes the relationship between language and experience from the opposite direction. He noted that "the formal schema is simply a system of second-degree operations and therefore a grouping operating on concrete groupings" (p. 152). The relationship between language and experience is a two-way street. As Helen Keller's account made clear, that experience makes sense only as it is shaped by language. Piaget points to the emptiness of language without a basis of experience. The developmental stage of concrete operations links the two. The more advanced stage of formal operations enables thought to develop as word structures build on word structures, constructions on constructions. Not only is communication impossible without language, but also even the ability to "think thoughts," as we normally consider it, is impossible without language.

Words enable the construction and communication of experience because they classify it. However, at the same time, words also shape (distort? destroy?) experience by simplifying and stabilizing it. The general semanticists, such as Alfred Korzybski (1958) and S. I. Hayakawa (1978), have made much of this. The word *penny* describes a group of objects that have one dominant characteristic in common: They represent a common unit of currency in our national monetary system. Beyond this, they are all generally brown, they are made of metal, they are shaped in circles, and they have two sides—generally designated as "heads" and "tails." But are they the same? Not really! They have different dates on them; they are at various stages of wear and corrosion; they all even have slightly different weights. Two pennies coined on the same day are not identical, even on the day that they are released from the mint. As the general semanticists would say, "Penny 1 is not penny 2." In the same way that words simplify the vast unstructured experience that is contained in all the pennies in the world, words also stabilize reality by ignoring changes that are constantly occurring in the objects we have classified. The Mississippi River is not the same body of water that it was 10 years ago, nor is Bill Smith the same person he was 10 years ago when he was a teenager. Both, in fact, have changed in many ways since yesterday. Yet, for most of our purposes, whether it be to make a purchase or toss a coin to make a decision, the term *penny* tells us everything that we really want to know. In the same way, *Bill Smith* (and the constructed realities that have grown up around that name) includes all the information that his family and friends need in order to relate to him. This is exactly the point! What we "want to know" and what we "need to know" determine the classification system we use to determine our language and thereby the construction of the reality with which each of us lives.

Low-level abstractions describe specific features of experience. They can be grouped into higher order abstractions, which, in turn, can be grouped into even higher order abstractions. For instance, "this dirty 1954 penny" can be classified under *pennies*, which can be included under the higher order abstraction of *coins*, which can then be classified under *money*. In the same way, *Bill Smith* can be classified under *men*, which can be classified under *people*. As we move up the abstraction ladder, categories become more and more inclusive, but the specificity of the original experience is increasingly lost.

In the same way that language constructs experience, it enables constructions to build on other constructions (what Piaget would identify as *formal operations*). As this occurs, the human mind devises ways of shaping experience that enable individuals to better adapt to it. Shared constructions provide the basis for communication between people, and shared experiences and communication about them generate additional shared constructions. The totality of shared constructions among a human group is the foundation of their language and their culture. When people attempt to communicate with other people, they face increasing difficulty as the number of shared constructions decreases.

The relationship between language and experience has important implications for our view of conducting research. Because we think in language and because words can never say everything about anything, our ability to interpret experience and to share it with others is limited to the capacity of these constructions. We can always learn more, and our constructions can help us learn more, but we can never learn everything, even if we had an infinite amount of time, because our language makes our experience intelligible by focusing only on limited aspects of it. If words and word structures did not construct reality, they would be useless. By shaping experience they screen out information that is not necessary for communication. They also make it difficult to communicate with persons whose experience has been shaped in drastically different ways.

For this reason, it is important for researchers to attempt to share the constructions of those whose human setting they are investigating. These shared constructions need not be identical; in fact, they cannot be. But they must be compatible so that communication can take place. Developing these compatible constructions will guide much of the naturalistic researcher's data collection and analysis. In the same way, the naturalistic researcher must take care to develop compatible constructions with the study's intended audience. As we will see, this is the same reason why the naturalistic researcher uses thick description. Low-level abstractions that provide descriptions—not of aggregated data, but of specific experiences —are used in abundance to keep descriptions as close as possible to the actual setting. It is thick description that will bring the reader vicariously into the setting the researcher is describing and thereby pave the way for shared constructions.

We are very impressed by the work of expert descriptive linguists whom we have observed (chiefly those who work with Wycliffe Bible Translators) and believe that what they do is very similar to the work of naturalistic researchers and can provide direction for them. On several occasions we have seen a linguist come into contact with a person whose language is totally unknown to the linguist. We have observed the linguist, using the tool of the phonetic alphabet and evoking words by pointing to objects, encouraging activities, and suggesting relationships, develop a communication with the person whose language had been previously unknown to the linguist. Because the demonstrations we have seen are generally quite short, we are amazed at how "fluent" the linguist appears to be in the previously unknown tongue in the space of half an hour. This, of course, is only the first step. Developing a written language and translating information into that language is a much longer process. The linguist will spend many hours with key native speakers, finding out the gentle nuances of their speech by eating, working, and playing with them and in teaching them to read their new written language. When the translation work is done, the linguist will launch into another long phase in which newly literate native speakers check the linguist's translation to determine if it evokes the images that, if not identical, are at least consistent with the ones in the original language. The process of building shared constructions is evident from the beginning to the end of the linguist's work.

The processes we will describe for building trustworthiness into a naturalistic study are strikingly similar to those used by the descriptive linguist who is engaged in developing a written language for a previously unknown spoken language. The linguist, like the naturalistic researcher, must somehow reconstruct the constructions of the respondent in such a way that the respondent can verify them. To do this, both linguist and naturalistic researcher must learn to step out of themselves so that they can view life through the eyes of the respondent. When their data have been reconstructed in a way acceptable to the respondent, they must then provide a translation or report that will enable similar constructions by others, not engaged in the original research, to benefit from it.

As people from different cultures and settings come into contact with each other, they begin to share their constructed realities with each other. This sharing is never a straightforward, clear communication of the original constructions; it is shaped by the host of realities already constructed by each group, based on their collective experiences as well as the relationships between the two groups. These shared constructions, in turn, do much to structure the future activities and relationships between the groups. Bauer (1992) notes this process as it has developed between the residents of the Spanish Sierra del Caurel and outsiders. On first visiting the region Bauer had this encounter with a group of the local women:

> Sweeping my hand over the field visible from the plaza, I remarked to this group, "You have a beautiful village here." Suddenly, an elderly woman dressed in the drab clothing of resident villagers rushed toward me from a

nearby porch where she had stood watching us approach. She shouted:
"You like this place? Well, you can have it. I'll trade you your place for
mine anytime. This place is ugly, and all we have here is hard work." (pp.
571-572)

As language shapes experience, shared constructions shape the relationships among individuals and groups. Bauer goes on to note how the
historical relationship between the natives of Caurel and outsiders, particularly members of Spain's ruling elites, have shaped images of self and
regional denigration for the Caurelaos. These images in turn govern the
relationships between Caurelaos and outsiders, and, in fact, are strategi-
cally used by the village spokesmen to document their own oppression
and abandonment by the state and, consequently, to gain advantages for
their community.

What Bauer noted regarding the relationship between Caurelaos and
outsiders provides insight regarding what happens whenever the constructed realities of separate cultures, settings, or even individuals come
into contact with each other. No person or group leaves such an encounter
with earlier constructions intact. The researcher is necessarily intrusive
upon the environment and persons being researched. In turn, he or she
cannot leave the research setting without new constructions of reality. The
deeper the understanding the researcher gains of the setting and the persons
in it, the more his or her own constructions will be affected. The naturalistic researcher, realizing this, does not attempt to insulate him or herself
from the setting but seeks to establish relationships through which the
mutual shaping of constructions is a collaborative exercise in which researcher and respondents voluntarily participate.

To the novice naturalistic researcher, and unfortunately to many experienced researchers as well, the question "Whose constructed realities are
the right ones?" becomes a critical issue. In this text we make several
references to William Whyte's classic sociological work, *Street Corner
Society* (1943). For 50 years this work has stood as a standard reference
for sociologists in urban settings. Yet Boelen (1992), many years later,
"revisited" Cornerville, talked to several of Whyte's original informants
and their families and developed an interpretation that rejected many of
Whyte's findings and called into question both the methodology and the
ethics of his study. The entire April 1992 issue of the *Journal of Contemporary Ethnography* is devoted to the debate between Whyte and Boelen
and includes commentary from other sociologists and from one of the
original participants in the Whyte study. It is hard to know which con-

structed realities are the right ones unless we know the context in which "right" is defined—in other words, "right for what purpose?" As Benjamin Whorf pointed out, the Hopi Indians' view of the universe seems wrong for most Westerners because it does not fit with the things they "know" to be right; yet it integrates very well with what the Hopis "know" about the world they experience.

Vidich (1992) makes a parallel observation about the Whyte-Boelen debate:

> The data evoked by the focus of the problem and its analysis become a reality in their own right: This is the observer-analyst's reality. That Boelen years later discovered informants in Cornerville who disagreed with Whyte's reality does not make Whyte's reality false or suspect but only recognizes that there is more than one reality. (p. 89)

Denzin (1992), writing in the same issue, chides both Whyte and Boelen for insisting that one interpretation is right and the other is wrong. He notes:

> [T]here is, in a sense, no final truth or final telling. There are only different tellings of different stories organized under the heading of the same tale; in this case, Bill Whyte's story of Cornerville. Now we have two different versions of the same story, and it becomes a different story in the new telling. (p. 124)

By insisting on a single reality and the need for proving their separate theories right or wrong, Denzin believes that both Whyte and Boelen demonstrate their adherence to a traditional epistemology that denies the legitimacy and worth of separate constructed realities and, by implication, the language, values, and conceptualizing principles of those who construct them.

In reflecting on the Whyte-Boelen debate, Richardson notes, "A continuing puzzle for me is how to do sociological research and how to write it so that the people who teach me about their lives are honored and empowered, even if they and I see their worlds differently" (1992, p. 108).

This is a compelling concern of the naturalistic researcher. Language is a precious possession. It affords a repository of the concepts that we use to organize our worlds and provides the tools with which we structure our experience. Because language is also a cultural phenomenon, it provides links with people in the same culture and with people across cultures. When I speak to a person in my own family, I can reasonably assume a large number of shared constructions (although even here I am often surprised by the discrepancies and ambiguities). When I reach out to persons of very different backgrounds, the development of shared constructions becomes a major first step in our relationship. If I am going to do research in a human setting, I must develop the shared constructions with my partners (respondents) in the setting. Only in this way will I, in Richardson's words, be able to "honor and empower" (1992, p. 108) those who have willingly let me enter their world and volunteered to teach me about it.

Building Trustworthiness

If intellectual inquiry is to have an impact on human knowledge, either by adding to an overall body of knowledge or by solving a particular problem, it must guarantee some measure of credibility about what it has inquired, must communicate in a manner that will enable application by its intended audience, and must enable its audience to check on its findings and the inquiry process by which the findings were obtained. Most readers are somewhat familiar with the way in which these concerns are ordinarily addressed by prevailing research methodology; these were alluded to briefly in Chapter 1. However, because we have been taught to esteem such methodology, we forget that our society has carefully decided, in some very important social arenas, to obtain, communicate, validate, and apply "truth" (or at least what is accepted for it) in alternative ways. In this chapter we will describe briefly the criteria that must be met for any research to be accepted as trustworthy. These criteria establish the foundation for the methods and procedures we will describe in the chapters that follow. In Chapter 7 we will again review how these criteria can be built into a naturalistic study.

For instance, we consider it a fundamental principle of our society that a person accused of a crime has a "right" to have his or her innocence or guilt decided by a jury of peers who listen to both the evidence that tends to confirm guilt and that which tends to disconfirm it. Also, the U.S. Supreme Court decides on the meaning of constitutional and legal provisions not through a scanning of multiple variables but by considering an intricate pattern of constitutional principles, previous court decisions, equity, and social impact. Or consider the way in which we elect the individuals who will govern us. "Truth" is defined by the greatest number of votes; it is verified by recounting the ballots if that is deemed necessary. In the "free market," a foundational base for our economic system, "truth" is negotiated by buyer and seller, neither of whom is considered to be an unbiased participant. (Consider in this context the demise of many socialist economies that sought to determine such "truth" through rational planning.) Yet all these accepted modes for solving real problems have certain things in common: They establish in advance (1) how "truth" will be determined (majority vote, jury decision, supply and demand), (2) how it will be communicated (majority opinion, verdict, price tag), and (3) how error will be detected and corrected (appeals process, future court decisions, price adjustments).

Do these procedures produce perfect answers to the problems they address? Absolutely not. Even the most unobservant member of our society can probably identify numerous occasions where each of these procedures has fallen short of the ideal answer or solution. Nevertheless, they have all persisted over many years. Seldom (with the earlier mentioned exception of the socialist challenge to the market determination of prices) has anyone seriously proposed that we replace these procedures with a rationalistic inquiry that would collect and analyze information in an unbiased manner that would produce objective "truth" with a defined probability of being correct. Yet this is precisely the encumbrance that we typically place on ourselves in conducting research in school organizations and other social settings.

However, valid inquiry in any sphere must be responsive to the concerns raised above. It must demonstrate its truth value, provide the basis for applying it, and allow for external judgments to be made about the consistency of its procedures and the neutrality of its findings or decisions. Guba and Lincoln have referred to these combined qualities as "trustworthiness," and have in their various writings described how trustworthiness can be assessed and strengthened in studies that follow the naturalistic paradigm (Guba, 1981; Guba & Lincoln, 1981; Guba & Lincoln, 1989; Lincoln & Guba, 1985). We shall use and develop their structures throughout this text as the basic means by which we believe trustworthiness can be built into naturalistic studies.

Credibility

A central question for any inquiry relates to the degree of confidence in the "truth" that the findings of a particular inquiry have for the subjects with which—and the context within which—the inquiry was carried out (Lincoln & Guba, 1985, p. 290). Within the prevailing research paradigm truth value is described in terms of internal validity, that is, the isomorphic relationship between the data of an inquiry and the phenomena those data represent. However, because naturalistic inquiry does not make the assumption of a single objective reality, the objective ascertainment of an isomorphism ceases to have any relevance. More pertinent is the compatibility of the constructed realities that exist in the minds of the inquiry's respondents with those that are attributed to them. This relationship is termed *credibility*.

Credibility needs to be established with the individuals and groups who have supplied data for the inquiry. It is assessed by determining whether the description developed through inquiry in a particular setting "rings true" for those persons who are members of that setting. Because these persons represent different constructed realities, a credible outcome is one that adequately represents both the areas in which these realities converge and the points on which they diverge. A credible inquiry generally has the effect on its readers of a mosaic image, often imprecise in terms of defining boundaries and specific relationships but very rich in providing depth of meaning and richness of understanding.

Because the major concern in establishing credibility is interpreting the constructed realities that exist in the context being studied and because these realities exist in the minds of the people in the context, attention must be directed to gaining a comprehensive intensive interpretation of these realities that will be affirmed by the people in the context. In their various writings, Guba and Lincoln have proposed a series of strategies for accomplishing this. They are briefly considered here and will be developed further in later chapters.

Prolonged Engagement. The researcher must spend enough time in the context being studied to overcome the distortions that are due to his or her impact on the context, his or her own biases, and the effect of unusual or seasonal events. "Enough" time in the context (culture) can be considered that amount that enables the researcher to understand daily events in the way that persons who are part of that culture (i.e., natives) interpret them.

Persistent Observation. However, while the researcher may be able to understand the events that occur and the relationships that exist in a social context in the same way that they are understood by a person who is part of that context, nothing is added to what could be told by any intelligent "native" unless the researcher can identify those events and relationships that are most relevant for solving a particular problem or resolving a particular issue. Such relevant depth can be obtained only by consistently pursuing interpretations in different ways in conjunction with a process of constant and tentative analysis.

Triangulation. Perhaps the best way to elicit the various and divergent constructions of reality that exist within the context of a study is to collect information about different events and relationships from different points of view. People in the context who are known to have distinctly different opinions and understandings of a topic should be deliberately sought out by the researcher. Data obtained directly from the statements of individuals should be checked against observed behavior and various records and documents. Different questions, different sources, and different methods should be used to focus on equivalent sets of data. Alternative explanations should be considered.

Referential Adequacy Materials. Because all data must be interpreted in terms of their context, it is extremely important that materials be collected to give holistic views of the context. Videotapes, documents, photographs, and any other materials that provide a "slice of life" from the context being studied will provide a supportive background that communicates to the reader a richer contextual understanding of the researcher's analyses and interpretations.

Peer Debriefing. Occasionally the researcher should step out of the context being studied to review perceptions, insights, and analyses with professionals outside the context who have enough general understanding of the nature of the study to debrief the researcher and provide feedback that will refine and, frequently, redirect the inquiry process.

Member Checks. Because the realities that will be included are those that have individually and collectively been constructed by persons within the context of the study, it is imperative that both data and interpretations obtained be verified by those persons. No data obtained through the study should be included in it if they cannot be verified through member checks.

Transferability

An inquiry is judged in terms of the extent to which its findings can be applied in other contexts or with other respondents (Lincoln & Guba, 1985, p. 290). Implementation of an inquiry's findings always requires an estimation of applicability because even if the inquiry in a particular context is meant only to guide decisions about the operation of that context in a succeeding time frame, time will change both the context and the individuals who are in it. For example, an evaluation study of the operation of a high school can be used to guide decisions for the following year only to the degree that the findings can be related to what that school is like in the following year. Every context shifts over time as the persons in that context, their constructions of reality, and the relationships among them also shift (even if the individuals are the same). When findings are applied across contexts, the problem of applicability increases. Some way must be found to either focus on those aspects of the inquiry that do not shift within or across contexts or to interpret findings in a way that makes allowance for the shift of context.

Most contemporary researchers view applicability in terms of generalizability and address the issue by focusing on those aspects of the inquiry that do not shift (or shift within the boundaries of probability) across contexts. Variations across contexts that cannot be linked to a systematic pattern (bias) are assumed to occur randomly and will fit a normal curve in their distribution. This is the reason for strict insistence on random selection from the target population; it enables generalizations across the population to be made within specified probabilities of error. The naturalistic researcher maintains, however, that no true generalization is really possible; all observations are defined by the specific contexts in which they occur.

The assumption of random variation merely means that the expected (not guaranteed) variation within an unbiased sample (if such can ever really be obtained) will be the same as the variation in the population. This works reasonably well for estimating simple parameters (e.g., voting preference), but when more complex estimates are made about complex interrelationships in a population (e.g., the web of factors that lead to voting preference), the differences between contexts are amplified, and generalizability rapidly breaks down.

The naturalistic researcher, however, does not maintain that knowledge gained from one context will have no relevance for other contexts or for the same context in another time frame. "Transferability" across contexts may occur because of shared characteristics. However, the basis for transferring knowledge emanates from a very different starting point. Rather than attempting to select isolated variables that are equivalent across contexts, the naturalistic researcher attempts to describe in great detail the interrelationships and intricacies of the context being studied. Thus the result of the study is a description that will not be replicated anywhere. The "thick description" that has been generated, however, enables observers of other contexts to make tentative judgments about applicability of certain observations for their contexts and to form "working hypotheses" to guide empirical inquiry in those contexts. This is an important distinction: In a traditional study it is the obligation of the researcher to ensure that findings can be generalized to the population; in a naturalistic study the obligation for demonstrating transferability belongs to those who would apply it to the receiving context (Guba & Lincoln, 1989, p. 241). With this in mind, two strategies are suggested here to facilitate transferability.

Thick Description. Because transferability in a naturalistic study depends on similarities between sending and receiving contexts, the researcher collects sufficiently detailed descriptions of data in context and reports them with sufficient detail and precision to allow judgments about transferability. Effective thick description brings the reader vicariously into the context being described. By description of specific sights, sounds, and relationships, the scene created in the reader's mind may be remarkably close to that which would be gained by direct experience. Often we have found that an individual whose first encounter with a setting is through an effective thick description has a sense of déjà vu upon actually visiting the setting.

Purposive Sampling. Because the foundation of transferability is an adequate description of the sending context, the search for data must be guided by processes that will provide rich detail about it. In contrast to the random sampling that is usually done in a traditional study to gain a representative picture through aggregated qualities, naturalistic research seeks to maximize the range of specific information that can be obtained from and about that context. This requires a sampling procedure that is governed by emerging insights about what is relevant to the study and purposively seeks both the typical and the divergent data that these insights suggest.

Dependability

An inquiry must also provide its audience with evidence that if it were replicated with the same or similar respondents (subjects) in the same (or a similar) context, its findings would be repeated (Lincoln & Guba, 1985, p. 290). The inquiry must meet the criterion of consistency.

In the prevailing research paradigm this quality is reflected in a concern for reliability, which refers to a study's (or instrument's) consistency,

predictability, stability, or accuracy. The establishment of reliability depends on replication, the assumption being made that repeated application
of the same or equivalent instruments to the same subjects under the same
conditions will yield similar measurements. Reliability is a precondition
for validity; there can be no assumption of an isomorphic relationship
between observations and reality if attempts at replication yield different
results (Guba & Lincoln, 1989, pp. 234-235).

The naturalistic researcher, however, believes that observed instability
may be attributed not only to error but also to reality shifts. Thus, the quest
is not for invariance but for "trackable variance" (Guba, 1981), variabili-
ties that can be ascribed to particular sources (error, reality shifts, better
insights, etc.). Consistency is conceived in terms of "dependability," a
concept that embraces both the stability implied by "reliability" and the
trackability required by explainable changes (Guba, 1981, p. 81). Dependability is communicated through a dependability audit.

Dependability Audit. To provide for a check on dependability, the researcher must make it possible for an external check to be conducted on
the processes by which the study was conducted. This is done by providing
an "audit trail" that provides documentation (through critical incidents,
documents, and interview notes) and a running account of the process
(such as the investigator's daily journal) of the inquiry.

Confirmability

Finally, an inquiry is judged in terms of the degree to which its findings
are the product of the focus of its inquiry and not of the biases of the
researcher (Lincoln & Guba, 1985, p. 290). Toward this end, the traditional researcher seeks to establish objectivity, which is guaranteed by
methodology that (1) is explicated, open to public scrutiny, and replicable
and (2) insulates observations from the biases of the researcher. The
naturalistic researcher, however, realizes that objectivity is an illusion and
that no methodology can be totally separated from those who have created
and selected it. The naturalistic researcher does not attempt to ensure that
observations are free from contamination by the researcher but rather to
trust in the "confirmability" of the data themselves. "This means that data
(constructions, assertions, facts, and so on) can be tracked to their sources,
and that the logic used to assemble the interpretations into structurally
coherent and corroborating wholes is both explicit and implicit" (Guba &

Lincoln, 1989, p. 243). Confirmability, like dependability, is communicated through an audit.

Confirmability Audit. The audit trail that was established to ascertain dependability by looking at the processes that were used in the study also enables an external reviewer to make judgments about the products of the study. An adequate trail should be left to enable the auditor to determine if the conclusions, interpretations, and recommendations can be traced to their sources and if they are supported by the inquiry.

A final word needs to be said about the importance of the audit trail in establishing trustworthiness for the naturalistic study. A useful parallel might be drawn here with the admonitions that have been given to guide traditional researchers. Just as there can be no external validity without internal validity, so there can be no transferability if credibility is lacking. Furthermore, as validity is meaningless unless reliability can be affirmed, in the same way credibility can be established only if dependability can be ensured. Finally, as objectivity (even by prevailing standards) is of no value unless it serves to guarantee something that itself has value, so confirmability can provide nothing greater than the value of what it confirms. For the naturalistic researcher these separate criteria are bound together through the audit trail. Further direction on construction of the audit trail is given in Chapter 7.

Selection of Methods

Much has been written and said about the respective merits of quantitative and qualitative methods for conventional and naturalistic-constructivist studies. In fact, the two paradigms are often classified by their methodologies: the conventional research paradigm as the quantitative paradigm and the naturalistic paradigm as the qualitative paradigm. We believe that such a classification is in error and unnecessarily confuses a very important issue. Mainstream researchers regularly use qualitative methods, and naturalistic researchers will often use quantitative methods. The operational differences between the two types of research are not so well defined by their different methodologies as by the reasons for which methods are selected and by how the data obtained from them are intended to be used.

Fred N. Kerlinger (1973, pp. 406, 483-484) presents rather clearly the way in which he values open-ended questions and relatively unstructured observations. Their purpose is to discover major relationships and patterns where little is known and to provide the basis for the more precise definition of variables and collection of categorized data. Once precisely categorized, the data can be manipulated and related statistically in various ways to other sets of data. The relationship between constructs is the source of "scientific" meaning.

Science traditionally has been considered to have two complementary aspects: discovery and verification. It seems that what Kerlinger attempts to do is to assign the discovery role to the naturalistic researcher and to reserve verification for traditional research. The naturalistic researcher cannot accept this limited role. The naturalistic researcher is as much concerned with verification as with discovery. Perhaps the biggest difference is that for the naturalistic researcher discovery and verification are intertwined with each other and cannot easily be contained in separate time or activity segments. It also seems likely that what Kerlinger is really concerned about is *generalizability*, a concept that the naturalistic researcher has already rejected.

In contrast with Kerlinger's prescription, the naturalistic researcher will sometimes use quantitative methods as a preliminary tool to obtain a quick picture of typical and atypical cases and a map of where the outliers may be found in order to facilitate further in-depth investigation. Sandra L. Bifano (1987) initiated her naturalistic study through administration of a quantitative instrument to a random sample of the 1,193 elementary school principals in a 61-county region. This sample was further reduced to those who expressed a willingness for a random sample of their teachers to complete an equivalent instrument. From these she identified schools that the measure indicated were outliers in different directions. Finally, after conducting on-site observations of several of these outliers to determine if the survey results reflected genuine operational differences, three schools were selected for in-depth naturalistic studies.

Note how this method mirrors that suggested by Kerlinger (p. 406), who would start with qualitative methods and work toward increasingly more precise quantitative measures. Bifano started with a quantitative method and worked toward unstructured observations and sorting out the rich and diverse unpredicted intricacies of three different contexts. This reversal of order and priority for the measures and the data they yield is a much better descriptor of the separate paradigms than are the measures themselves.

Bifano used a quantitative measure to obtain a broad preliminary picture of divergent possibilities in her search for settings that would be suitable for her study. Quantitative measures can be used in a similar manner within a setting in order to facilitate the search for sources that will provide information on its typical and unusual characteristics. For instance, a paper-and-pencil personality inventory administered to all the members of an organization may provide the naturalistic researcher with another tool in selecting a purposive sample. Other examples of how quantitative as well as qualitative instruments may be selected to serve the purposes of a naturalistic study will be provided elsewhere in this text.

However, this order of using quantitative measures followed by qualitative measures, as demonstrated in the Bifano study, does not by itself distinguish naturalistic studies from more conventional research. It is quite possible, for example, to start with a quasi-experimental design and then use qualitative data to test alternative rival hypotheses that are generated by it. What is crucial here is not the order of the methods but whether the combined measures are designed to reduce or expand the constructions of reality that are being considered.

Kimberly A. Klint (1988) conducted two studies of motivation in young girl gymnasts, one of which followed the prevailing paradigm and the other the naturalistic paradigm. Her comparison of the two studies reflected fairly well the assumptions and priorities of the two paradigms. It should be noted that Klint's studies were not really parallel, because the paradigmatic assumptions of the studies were so different. Similarly, the results of the studies could not be compared. The two studies, however, did a good job of communicating the types of questions that are addressed by the two paradigms and the types of information that each provides. She noted, for instance, that the readers of the more traditional study would ideally come away with the same understandings as the researcher but that this could not be said for the naturalistic study because the thick description allowed and invited a much more active role for the reader. She noted also that a researcher using the prevailing paradigm may gain rich insights in the process of conducting the inquiry, but that she is usually barred from sharing these with her readers in a meaningful way unless they are directly related to the original research questions. She noted that although the findings of the traditional study "may represent a multi-faceted jewel, all these facets will not necessarily be available to the readers" (Klint, p. 201). The same barriers did not apply in her naturalistic study.

She also noted a relationship between the two types of studies reflective of the one we noted in relation to the Bifano study:

> Suppose each respondent's reality is represented by a set of colored tiles. The overlaying of these tiles creates a mosaic-type picture, where some

colors and patterns converge to form fairly discrete lines and forms. In other areas, the colors and patterns from each individual reality only form diffuse, and seemingly shapeless, forms. The naturalist sees the positivist as trying to capture the essence of one part of the mosaic through a crude drawing. A shapeless form is described by a single line; red and blue tiles may be represented by the color purple. The end result is a drawing [that] may not communicate the essence of the final mosaic. Additionally, this drawing may not be found in any one of the individual patterns [that] compose the final mosaic. Thus, the relationship between the two sets of knowledge arising from both paradigms cannot be consistently defined. (p. 206)

Thus, although there is no reason why quantitative measures cannot be used in naturalistic inquiry (and they often are), there are important reasons why qualitative measures are generally preferred. Quantitative measures seek always to reduce data to numbers that represent a single criterion. By so doing they remove those data from the rich detail that distinguish them from other similar data and from the contexts and alternative constructions that give them meaning. Quantitative measures present abstractions that destroy much of the detail that enables shared constructions, communicates credibility to persons in the contexts from which the data were taken, and provides the basis for transferability through thick description.

Data Collection and Analysis

The different assumptions of the prevailing and naturalistic-constructivist paradigms also lead to a key difference in the way in which data collection and data analysis are related in a study. Klint was able to perform her separate studies over the same period of time because of these different characteristics. Because the "rules" of traditional inquiry required her data collection procedures to be uncontaminated by the researcher, she was able to collect (and then store) them without becoming aware of what they revealed. She was then able to conduct her naturalistic study, including a period of prolonged engagement in which she conducted interactive (and often simultaneous) data collection and analysis. After she had completed her naturalistic study, she was able to return to the stored, uncontaminated data of her traditional study and analyze them according to the procedures prescribed by her preordinate design. While these procedures enabled her to retain the "purity" of the study, they also prevented her from tapping the most fertile and significant insights that were present in the settings of her study.

The realization that objectivity in research is an illusion frees the naturalistic researcher to do truly effective data collection and analysis. Most important is the fact that the researcher him- or herself becomes the most significant instrument for data collection and analysis. Addition of the human computer (an instrument unsurpassed for the flexible acquisition and analysis of diverse and simultaneous data) to the researcher's inventory of tools provides advantages that far outweigh the supposed disadvantages, even if the case for objectivity in research could be sustained.

The human instrument allows data to be collected and analyzed in an interactive process. This, of course, merely follows the normal process by which humans solve their daily problems. As soon as data are obtained, tentative meaning is applied to them. When new data are obtained, meaning is revised. Obviously, some people are better problem solvers than others, and one of the major factors that makes them so is their ability to revise analyses based on new and emerging data. Traditional restrictions to ensure objectivity seem to be directed at neutralizing the differences in observational and analytical abilities among researchers by making them largely nonoperational. The naturalistic researcher attempts to develop and maximize the observational and analytical abilities of the researcher by utilizing them in situations that provide feedback on their efficacy. This theme will be emphasized throughout the text.

Another way that naturalistic inquiry is different from traditional inquiry in methods of data collection and analysis comes from the lack of a preordinate design or established procedures to follow. The traditional researcher knows before data collection begins exactly what data will be collected, how they will be stored, and how they will be retrieved; the naturalistic researcher lacks this advantage. However, from the very beginning the naturalistic researcher struggles to infer from the context an overall, though tentative, design that will provide direction for subsequent data collection and analysis. Though this initial design will be modified and refined many times over the course of the inquiry, its value as a guide for data collection, analysis, and retrieval cannot be overestimated. As such, it lays the foundation for the audit trail.

The audit trail, though providing its main utility after the study has been completed, must be considered from the beginning. More than one researcher has lost valuable pieces of this audit trail because he or she did not provide for this requirement from the beginning of the study. As a general consideration, it is better, particularly in the early stages of the study, to retain too many notes and documents rather than too few. An emerging design provides increasing efficiency to the process and enables the systematic collection of material for the audit trail.

Reporting the Inquiry

One of the characteristics of naturalistic inquiry is that it empowers the various people who are involved in it. We have already noted that the credibility of a study is essentially its ability to communicate the various constructions of reality in a setting back to the persons who hold them in a form that will be affirmed by them. In Chapter 8 we shall discuss the need for negotiating the outcomes of a naturalistic study with stakeholders in the context. In the same manner the user (reader) of the study should be empowered through the report of the inquiry.

We have already noted how the thick description of a naturalistic study allows and invites an active role for the reader. We have also seen that the primary burden for transferability to another context is on those who would apply it to the receiving context. The obligation of the researcher in writing the report is to produce a document that will allow for active participation on the part of the reader and provide the basis for developing working hypotheses that can be applied in other contexts.

Lincoln and Guba (1985, pp. 357-360) have proposed that the case study, accompanied by a methodological report, is the reporting mode of choice for the naturalistic study. This contrasts with the conventional reporting format, associated with traditional studies, that moves from research questions or hypotheses to the design of the study (including instruments and statistical tools that will be used in the study), to a statement of the findings in terms of the original hypotheses and questions, to a statement of conclusions and recommendations. The conventional report operates within the limits of the research questions and design and, at least until recommendations are given at the end of the report, is confined to data that are directly responsive to them. By contrast, the case study allows for thick description that puts the reader vicariously into the context and allows him or her to interact with the data presented. It should be realized, of course, that the reader cannot make an entirely independent judgment; to some degree, as in every study, the reader's comprehension is shaped by the explicit and implicit priorities and judgments of the researcher. However, in a well-done naturalistic study the reader, by being allowed to interact with the data in their total context, will be encouraged to extend the researcher's analysis to greater depth and in new directions.

This requires a level of skill in writing that is not usually required in a conventional research report. The ability to put a reader vicariously in a setting is usually associated with the highest levels of literary ability and is not generally found among persons who do research. If such skill were required for every naturalistic study, not many would be completed or even begun. The purpose of this book is to encourage, not discourage, such studies. Nevertheless, by noting the value of such writing ability for the author of the naturalistic report, we would like to encourage all who would write such reports to note this priority on writing skill and to work consciously on developing such skill to ensure that their studies are not emasculated by the form in which they are communicated.

For Further Study

1. Read Hollingshead (1975), Lortie (1975), Whyte (1943), Wolcott (1973), or some other book-length anthropological or sociological study that was published before 1980. Note where the researcher has followed traditional procedures for ensuring trustworthiness and where he or she has followed procedures more appropriate to naturalistic inquiry. Make judgments about how suitable the methods and procedures were for the purpose of the study. Then compare your notes with others who have read other selections. Could these studies have been improved through different methodology? Note that these studies were done prior to the formalization of the naturalistic (constructivist) paradigm; consider how they might have been different if they had consciously followed the new paradigm.

2. Read Kuhn (1970) and Chapters 1 and 2 of Lincoln and Guba (1985). Come to a reasoned conclusion about whether the shift from positivism truly represents a paradigm shift in the Kuhnian sense. Discuss your conclusion with others who have gone through the same process.

3. Think back to the "portraits" by Lightfoot (1983) that you examined in Chapter 1. Is Lightfoot's work transferable? Defend your answers.

4. Consider the naturalistic study that you began to plan in Chapter 1. Provide the best tentative answers that you can to the basic questions you have formulated. On what evidence do you base these answers? Where will you obtain this information? What follow-up questions are suggested? What additional basic questions are suggested?

3

≡

Getting Started on the Study

A CHINESE PROVERB SAYS, "A journey of a thousand miles begins with a single step." One of the most difficult aspects of conducting any type of research is to get started, to take the first step. The task of completing a dissertation or other significant study is so monumental that some aspiring researchers never begin the process and many never finish. However, if one takes the charge one step at a time, the probability of success dramatically increases. The process begins by identifying a problem that will provide direction for the study. Once identified, even in nebulous terms, the researcher can begin to look for a site where the problem can be researched. In some cases the problem and site will emerge at the same point. Either the researcher or someone else will be confronted by a problem in a particular social context that needs additional understanding, and the researcher will begin to focus on that particular problem. Once the problem has been identified and the site has been identified, the problem will continue to be refined. The problem does not stand in a contextual vacuum; it has meaning only in a particular social context. In a naturalistic study, because the definition of the problem is embedded in the constructed realities of the various stakeholders and the researcher cannot possibly know them in advance, problem definition and refinement continue for some time after the study has started. Nevertheless, the purpose of this chapter is to help the researcher get through the beginning stages of problem identification and site selection that will frame the nature of his or her study.

Identifying a Problem

The range of potential problems for research in human contexts is extremely broad and diverse. How does one find a researchable problem? How are problems for a naturalistic study stated? These important questions are common to researchers and must be answered before any inquiry begins.

Any competent real estate salesperson will say that there are three important characteristics of good property: "Location, location, location!" In research, three criteria that should follow the project throughout its entirety are "Interest, interest, interest!" The first question that must be asked and serve as a guide in many decisions concerning problem identification is "What are the researcher's interests?" Relevance, timeliness, feasibility, and other considerations are vital in the selection of a research problem. However, the completion of a successful research project could be hindered if the researcher is not intrigued with the problem, despite its significance or feasibility. In studying a human context, this means that the researcher has a passion to get behind the mediating words that initially link the researcher with the context and to construct shared realities with the human beings in that context. The authors of this book represent a wide range of interests, and each has pursued research problems that have evoked this passion. Good research is hard work, taxing, and time-consuming. If one planned to spend the next year (or longer) with one person, he or she would want that person to be exciting, stimulating, interesting, and compatible. The naturalistic researcher will invest an extended period of time on his or her study, and interest in the problem may be what sustains the researcher through the months or years of demanding labor.

As defined by Lincoln and Guba (1985), a problem is a state of affairs that (1) begs for additional understanding, (2) identifies the need for choosing between alternative courses of action, or (3) leads to undesirable consequences. "The purpose of a research inquiry is to 'resolve' the problem in the sense of accumulating sufficient knowledge to lead to understanding or explanation, a kind of dialectical process that plays off the thetical and antithetical propositions that form the problem into some kind of synthesis" (pp. 226-227).

An important aspect of arriving at a research problem is to seek help from a competent, experienced researcher. If the aspiring researcher is a graduate student, the chairperson of his or her dissertation committee is the likely candidate. It would be beneficial to jot some general interests on a sheet of paper and schedule a meeting with the chairperson. From these interests should come several broad ideas that could serve as a basis of conversation. For example, if one has a broad interest in athletics, he or she might come to the first meeting with several tentative questions: "How do women's attitudes influence their athletic performance?" or "Why do men lift weights?" These broad and open questions can lead to all sorts of specific problems such as: "What dynamics exist in the attitude and performance of the women in the university who are successful in track and field?" or "How do men in this apartment building who work out feel about themselves in comparison to those who do not?"

The dialogue between student and professor or between one colleague and another helps to clarify and narrow the focus of study. Also there are times when the chairperson or colleague is doing research in a similar area of interest and might welcome a graduate student or other researcher assisting on part of the project. Strauss and Corbin (1990) comment: "This way of finding a problem tends to increase the possibility of getting involved in a 'doable' and 'relevant' research problem. This is because the more experienced researcher already knows what has been done and needs to be done in a particular substantive area" (p. 84).

Again, remember the important criterion of interest. If one chooses to collaborate on a project, it is vital that he or she is genuinely intrigued with the proposed project in order to do an adequate job for oneself and for the experienced researcher.

Another source for research problems is the professional literature. What does the research say in the area of your interests? An important part of reading the current literature is that it helps the researcher find out what problems are significant. The significance of a problem lies in its time-liness, originality, and importance, as well as its academic and practical values. Keeping abreast of the professional literature guards the researcher from unnecessary duplication of trivial or poorly designed previous works and allows him or her to foresee significant directions and issues.

The research of the literature can also reveal those areas in former research that can be expanded or amplified. Expansion is similar to the term *replication* in conventional research, but there are significant differences in the purpose for building on a previous study in naturalistic research. The important concepts of generalizability and transferability, which are discussed in Chapters 2 and 7, come into play here. It is the belief in conventional research that time and context-free generalizations can provide the foundations for a priori hypotheses. For example, if a certain hypothesis is accepted as probable in one study, a researcher can repeat the first researcher's investigation in order to see if it yields the same results. If the results are the same, then confidence is strengthened in the hypothesis. If different results are obtained, then this calls into question errors in one or both of the studies and suggests limits on the generalizability of the findings in the first study.

The naturalistic inquirer operates under a different set of assumptions concerning the nature of reality, epistemology, and generalizability. The aim of naturalistic inquiry is not to develop a body of knowledge in the form of generalizations that are statements free from time or context. The aim is to develop shared constructions that illuminate a particular context and provide working hypotheses for the investigation of others. The purpose, then, for a naturalistic researcher conducting a study similar to a previous one is not to yield the same results, disclose errors in former methodology, or to strengthen the generalizability to the universe. Rather, it is primarily to expand on the processes and constructed realities of one study to seek initial illumination of the context of another study. For this reason *expansion research* is used in lieu of the traditional term of *replication*. For the naturalistic researcher, expansion research may serve the following purposes.

1. *Expansion research may examine the credibility or transferability of the constructed realities found in one setting in a different setting.* For example, one of the authors conducted a study that was a partial expansion of a previous work concerning espoused theories and actual professional practices of elementary school principals (Allen, 1990). The author's study utilized some of the same methods and logic as the original work. However, he contributed to the body of knowledge by providing insights into the professional practices of high school principals, and the latter research was conducted at two completely different sites than the former study.

Similarly, Shapira and Navon (1991) extended research that had been done on "third places" in the United States to similar settings in Israel:

> Ambiguous settings such as the cafe provide especially interesting arenas for the examination of social behavior, since they allow complex processes of negotiation, manipulation, and adaptation to occur. Therefore, it should be no surprise that leisure places [such as bars, pubs, and coffeehouses] have [been] extensively investigated by various researchers. . . . Nevertheless, these studies have been, for the most part, conducted in, and related to, the cultural context of the United States. An examination of social definitions within "third places" in a different cultural milieu should provide an enlightening perspective on universal and cultural-specific meanings of public and private realms.

Israel reveals itself as a particularly suitable context for such an enterprise. First, . . . [Israeli] society has different definitions of public and private spaces from those prevalent in the [United States]. Second, Israel is sprinkled with "third places" such as coffeehouses, whose outward appearance bears close resemblance to the parallel establishments analyzed in the American literature. (p. 108)

2. *Expansion research may investigate findings using different methodologies.* There are a plethora of studies that have been conducted using conventional quantitative methodology. Many of the topics researched in these studies are very timely, and a scan of these studies may suggest that understanding of the topics needs to be expanded through naturalistic studies. The assumptions and stance of naturalistic inquiry can add insight into perennial problems that simply cannot be attained through the conventional model. It can allow educators to look at problems through new windows. Jane Goodall (1990) explains:

There are many windows through which we can look out into the world, searching for meaning. There are those opened up by science, their panes polished by a succession of brilliant penetrating minds. . . . But there are other windows. . . [M]ost of us . . . peer through but one of those windows . . . and even that one is often misted over by the breath of our finite humanity. No wonder we are often confused. . . . It is . . . like trying to comprehend the panorama of the desert or the sea through a rolled-up newspaper. (p. 10)

We would caution the researcher, however, that even though we advocate the combination of methods, we are not advocating the combination of paradigms. A paradigm is a way of looking at the world, and it is very difficult to combine it with another paradigm that advocates a contradictory way of looking at the world. The traditional paradigm seeks to communicate by reducing meaning to discrete terms. The naturalistic paradigm seeks to communicate by expanding meaning, even if new meaning conflicts with former knowledge. This is why, though the naturalistic researcher will always look at knowledge obtained through alternative methods, the incorporation of a paradigm that reduces meaning is inherently counterproductive.

3. *Expansion research may examine changes over time.* Educational institutions are dynamic, animate, changing environments. What might have "worked" or been effective several years ago may or may not be

appropriate today. Naturalistic inquiry takes into account the dynamics and complexities of a changing society and can be valuable in determining today's transferability and dependability of previous research findings.

Still another source of research problems is contemporary societal trends and issues. Many societal issues can be construed as research problems appropriate for educators to investigate. For example, the feminist movement raised questions about sex equity and sex stereotyping of educational materials and practices. The civil rights movement led to research on the education of minority children and segregation (Merriam, 1988). Sources for determining and identifying societal trends and issues include professional seminars and journals, newspapers, television documentaries, news magazines, and college courses.

Personal capabilities and professional experience should be taken into consideration in determining a research problem. If the researcher has an extensive background in special education, then he or she is probably familiar with the many problems associated in that field. On the other hand, if the researcher has no experience whatsoever in special education, then it might not be advisable to take on a topic in that complex area. The difficulties of constructing shared realities with persons in a setting are intensified if the researcher does not have the necessary experience to construct realities that are compatible with those persons' constructed realities. Many aspiring researchers have embarked on significant projects only to find that when they reached the analysis stage they lacked the necessary skills or background to satisfactorily continue the study. According to Strauss and Corbin (1990):

> Choosing a research problem through the professional or personal experience route may seem more hazardous than through the suggested or literature routes. This is not necessarily true. The touchstone of your own experience may be more valuable an indicator for you of a potentially successful research endeavor. (pp. 35-36)

Occasionally, personal experience and social trends converge to generate an appropriate topic for study. Knowles (1991) provides an illustration of this:

> As a result of my professional preparation as a school teacher and as a parent, I was acutely aware of the benefits of parental interest and participation in

children's educational development. In the late 1970s, while working in a geographically isolated location in the South Pacific, my two children were unable to attend a formal school. To resolve the problem, we devised a home-based educational program. In the mid-1980s, I taught a summer school university class on the topic of outdoor education for parents. Based on the success of the class, I was invited to give workshops at the 1985 annual convention of the Utah Home Educational Association. As a result of these initial contacts with the home school community, I established a measure of rapport that allowed relatively easy access to many home schools. (pp. 206-207)

Knowles goes on to describe how his personal expertise and his contacts with the rapidly growing home school movement led to his study to identify and understand parents' rationales for operating home schools.

An obvious thing to keep in mind is the feasibility of studying the problem. You may have an interest in Japanese secondary education, but if you are living on a graduate assistant stipend, have a limited travel budget, and have no knowledge of the Japanese language, then it clearly would not be feasible to tackle such a topic. Feasibility considerations include finances, other individuals involved, transportation, geographical flexibility, family, and choosing an appropriate site.

If the researcher is a student, then it is important to consider future career goals and not simply generate a thesis or dissertation for graduation purposes. The doctoral student's final research project is often referred to as a "calling card," because it serves to provide the base for the researcher's reputation and published articles, as well as the springboard for professional growth and opportunities. Thus the process involved in the selection of a significant problem is all the more important.

It is important to acquire the attitude of a learner in conversations, reading, determining the significance of the study, making decisions concerning expansion, and assessing one's own capabilities and career goals. If the researcher approaches his or her study with the attitude of self-sufficiency and expertise, then the study will be limited. The researcher should question concepts and procedures, follow clues and recommendations, strive to think critically and challenge statements made in the professional literature. It is good to cultivate the habit of carrying a reflective journal to daily record notes and ideas. The researcher should continue this reflective writing practice throughout the entire research process.

Stating Research Problems and Questions

Once the researcher has defined a general problem, the specific problem can be defined. Focusing on a specific problem statement serves two major purposes:

> First, such focusing establishes the boundaries for a study; it defines the terrain, as it were, that is to be considered the proper territory of the inquiry. . . . Second, such focusing effectively determines the inclusion-exclusion criteria for new information that comes to light. The naturalist, even with inquiry boundaries quite firmly in mind, is likely, because earlier stages of an inquiry are conducted with wider sweeps of the data collection net, to dredge up much information that . . . is not relevant. Focusing helps the naturalist . . . make the decision to retain or discard information. (Lincoln & Guba, 1985, pp. 227-228)

The problem statement in naturalistic research is not a question or even an objective, but rather, as we have noted, an expression of a dilemma or situation that needs to be addressed for the purposes of understanding and direction. The purpose of a research inquiry is to seek to resolve the problem by accumulating pertinent knowledge and information and, in collaboration with the various stakeholders in the social context being studied, construct meaning directed toward that end.

Although the purpose of expansion research is not to disclose errors in previous studies, apparent incongruities in previous research may present the researcher with a problem that will give initial direction to the study. For instance, on reading Whyte's classic study *Street Corner Society* (1943), Boelen (1992) questioned some of Whyte's inferences and constructions. Having lived for four years in Italy and having observed young men habitually congregating on street corners, she questioned whether what Whyte saw as "gang formation" was not simply a pattern carried over from Italy and continued among young Italian men in the United States.

As a rule of thumb, the problem statement should be sufficiently broad to permit inclusion of central issues and concerns, and yet it should be narrow enough in scope to serve as a guide to data collection.

Helmer (1991) provides this statement, which guided him in his analysis of the culture of harness racing:

> The aim of this research is to penetrate the world of the backstretch and explore one important source of social cohesion and meaning—the horse

itself. "A horse," Mead observes in one of his examples, "is not simply something that must be ridden. It is an animal that must eat, that belongs to somebody. It has economic values" (1934, p. 12). In the backstretch it also has psychological and social values. Like the rodeo participants described by Lawrence (1982), the people of the backstretch constitute a pastoral society in which human relationships with animals are fundamental to a variety of significant social phenomena. The goals of this study, then, are to describe the unique local culture (Geertz, 1983) of the backstretch and analyze how the horse not only influences local systems of meaning but also how the horse itself constitutes the focus of a cultural system. (pp. 175-176)

After the problem has been adequately stated, the next step is to develop the research questions. Naturalistic inquiry relies on theory that emerges from the data (i.e., a posteriori) rather than precedes them (i.e., a priori). The research questions, then, should be phrased in such a way that allows the researcher to develop and explore theory that emerges from the context under study. A basic categorization scheme for these types of questions is the *who, what, where, how,* and *why* type. Yin (1984) elaborates:

Defining the research questions is probably the most important step to be taken in the research study, so patience and sufficient time should be allowed for this task. The key is to understand that research questions have both substance—for example, What is my study about?—and form—for example, Am I asking a "who," "what," "where," "why" or "how" question? (p. 19)

Generally speaking, *who, what,* and *where* questions may either be exploratory (e.g., What are the general patterns of behavior that characterize the principals of the three schools? Where does learning take place?) or predictive (e.g., What are the outcomes of the new program? Who is responsible for this change?). In contrast, *how* and *why* questions are more explanatory and deal with operational links that need to be traced over time (e.g., Why do fights occur in the school?) (Yin, 1984).

An important role of the research question is to establish boundaries on what will be studied. In naturalistic research there are a magnitude of investigative possibilities. The research questions aid the inquirer in narrowing the research problem to a manageable size. However, there is a delicate balance between narrowing the focus of the inquiry and allowing for the possibility of innovation and flexibility while conducting the study. Strauss and Corbin (1990) speak to this issue:

While the initial question starts out broadly, it becomes progressively narrowed and more focused during the research process, as concepts and their relationships are discovered to be relevant or irrelevant. So, the research question begins as an open and broad one; but not so open . . . as to allow for the entire universe of possibilities. Yet not so narrow and focused that it excludes discovery. . . . The research question in a grounded theory study is a statement that identifies the phenomenon to be studied. It tells you what you specifically want to focus on and what you specifically want to know about the subject. [They] also tend to be oriented toward process and action. (p. 38)

As noted, the research questions are interrelated with and should complement the research problem. The following are examples of research problems and their corresponding questions.

Research Problem 1

The [1980s] saw an unprecedented cry for educational reform. . . . These problems suggest the need to investigate the dynamics of principal-teacher interactions and develop methods for increasing involvement of professional educators in the total operation of our schools. (Allen, 1990)*

The researcher in this case, having identified two schools that seemed to offer contrasting settings for examination of the identified problem, formed three questions that provided direction for collecting data directed toward understanding the nature of the principal-teacher interactions that occurred in each school and their impact on the social context of the school.

Research Questions

1. What are the interactions between principals and teachers that occur in the school of the principal who has demonstrated a disposition to clearly define and achieve goals for the operation of the school?
2. What are the interactions between principals and teachers that occur in the school of the principal who has demonstrated a disposition to maximize valid information in the operation of the school?
3. How may the learning and organizational cultures of the schools in the study be described?

Research Problem 2

Culture has emerged as a pervasive explanation of why some schools are more successful than others. However, difficulty in examining school culture arises from the lack of readily available instruments. The problem is how to make something so powerful, but difficult to quantify, reveal itself. (Skipper, 1989)

In this case the researcher wished to understand as fully as possible the culture of a school that was considered by many observers to be a "good high school." Her initial questions were guided by this purpose to first identify the behavior patterns evident in the high school that typified and communicated its culture. She also sought to open the constructions of the various stakeholders of the setting by asking them to identify and share the metaphors with which they characterized the school. Finally, she wished to identify who in the setting were the chief builders and communicators of the culture. This led her to three questions.

Research Questions

1. What are the patterns of behavior that characterize the culture of Randolph High School?
2. What metaphors best describe the culture of Randolph High School?
3. Who promotes and perpetuates the culture of the school?

Research Problem 3

The transmission of moral values has been one of public education's oldest missions and is currently one of its newest sources of conflict. Contemporary educators are charged with educating a more culturally complex student population than ever before, and there is a lack of systematic data as to how much and in what ways value issues can be presented. The field of education needs an approach to moral education that takes into account pluralistic atmospheres and that can be effectively integrated into the curriculum and culture of the school. (Harris, 1991)

In this study the researcher sought to identify, compare, and contrast the patterns by which two very different schools (one public and rural, the other Jewish and urban), both with reputations for emphasizing values in their educational programs, clarified and communicated values in their schools and integrated them into their educational programs. This led to four initial questions.

Research Questions

1. How are values presented and practiced in the schools studied?
2. Who primarily instigates the integration of values in each school?
3. What roles do the teachers, students, and principals play in this process?
4. Where does values education take place?

Developing the research problem and formulating questions that lead the researcher to vital data require much preparation. Early investments of time and attention to this process will yield many profitable returns when the researcher becomes overwhelmed by the mountains of data to be analyzed in the research process.

Selecting a Site

The selection of a suitable site is a critical decision in naturalistic research, because the inquirer will conduct his or her study in a particular native setting to observe and record the day-to-day operations of the environment. Furthermore, the data collected in the research are limited to the selected site and its immediate context. Site selection affects the viability of the whole study, and great attention should be given to this process.

Will any site suffice for a particular study? Is there an ideal setting? First and foremost, having identified a research problem that is significant and that promises to engage the continuing interest of the researcher, the researcher is compelled to identify a site that maximizes the opportunity to engage that problem. Once this is ascertained, other considerations help determine the relative feasibility of alternative sites. Marshall and Rossman (1989) note:

> The ideal site is where (1) entry is possible; (2) there is a high probability that a rich mix of many of the processes, people, programs, interactions, and/or structures that may be a part of the research question will be present; (3) the researcher can devise an appropriate role to maintain continuity of presence for as long as necessary; and (4) data quality and credibility of the study are reasonably assured by avoiding poor sampling decisions. (p. 54)

One should not confuse the term *ideal* with *perfect*. A utopian setting is nonexistent. However, there are some sites better or more suitable than others. The researcher should seek to find the best site possible within the boundaries of his or her resources, and the primary guides for site selection are the specific research topic problem and questions. For example, if the problem concerns the planned implementation of values education, then it is important to select an educational institution that strives to integrate a value dimension into its educational program. In contrast, if the problem concerns broad implications of school-home communication, then the research might be conducted in almost any school organization and in multiple sites.

There are several ways to initially go about sifting through the milieu of possible site alternatives and narrowing the focus of the study to the best location(s). One way is through the survey questionnaire. One's research problem might generate several questions that can be sent to many school districts. From the responses to these survey questions, the researcher can make initial decisions concerning the viability of each possible site. One of the authors used this method in selecting a site for his study. The research problem emphasized the need to investigate the dynamics of principal-teacher interaction and to develop methods for increasing involvement of professional educators in the total operation of public schools. The site selection process was conducted in two primary phases:

Phase One—In this phase, principals of Class AAAA and Class AAAAA Texas High Schools were asked to respond to a series of scenarios dealing with principal-teacher interaction. Each item on the questionnaire consisted of a statement of a hypothetical situation followed by a four point Likert-type response. Items were of the format, "In this situation, I would. . . . " The principal's responses to the survey instrument provided a working hypothesis of each principal's espoused theory of leadership.

Phase Two—In this phase, the researcher made site visits and conducted interviews with two principals who had strong contrasting styles of leadership. Utilizing a qualitative interview approach, the researcher determined that the principals' professional practices appeared to be consistent with the theories they espoused in their survey responses. Based upon that determination, those schools were selected for the naturalistic research. (Allen, 1990)

Another way of selecting a site is through dialogue, interviews, and conversation with other professionals who have knowledge of the subject matter of your study. An example of this is given in the following excerpt from a dissertation on values education:

> The study was conducted during the spring semester of the 1989-90 school year. Prior to this time the researcher spent approximately six months speaking with school administrators, university professors, graduate students, and other educators in order to select two schools [that] strive to integrate a value dimension into their respective school cultures. [Two schools] were [finally] selected because of their reputation for integrating values education in their educational programs, and because of the principals' emphasis on values in each school.
>
> Interviews were conducted with the principal of each school in order to verify that these sites would be appropriate, to gain permission for entree, and to establish trust between researcher and respondents. Both principals expressed interest in participating in the inquiry and dates were agreed upon for the site visits to be conducted.
>
> Permission to proceed in the inquiries was obtained from the appropriate personnel in each school system. (Harris, 1991)

Lightfoot (1983) offers insight into her site selection process.

> [W]e searched for goodness—exemplary schools that might tell us something about the myriad definitions of educational success and how it is achieved. Second, we wanted diversity among the secondary schools—diversity of philosophies, resources, populations, and types. And third, we were eager for geographic representation. Our selection was not scientific. No random sample was taken, no large-scale opinion surveys were sent out in order to identify good schools. They were chosen because of their reputation among school people, the high opinion of them shared by their inhabitants and surrounding communities, and because they offered easy and generous entry. (p. 11)

In a study by one of the authors, a similar process was employed to select a site. A superintendent who heard about her endeavors offered her a position as a counselor in the high school in his district so that she could write the study as a participant-observer. An offer for such generous entry into a school, accepted in the local community as a good high school, could not be easily refused. By accepting a participant-observer role, she was able to get inside the culture of the school and become part of it. Although her role as a researcher was never covert, her role as a counselor in the school was (and, probably more important, was perceived as) her paramount reason for being in the school. Firsthand she was able to experience and record how the participants in the system react not to an outside researcher but rather to a new member of the system. Whether to be in a participative or nonparticipative role in the system is a decision that must be made by the researcher.

Whether the researcher uses one or a combination of the above methods, there are certain considerations that are generic to site selection for a naturalistic study. In each of these considerations one must remember the guiding rule that the selection process should be interrelated with and directed by the research problem.

A major consideration is accessibility. Can the researcher obtain access? Marshall and Rossman (1989) comment:

> A site may be perfect for generalizability, for interest, and for its range of examples of the phenomena under study, but if the researcher cannot gain access to the site and to the range of groups and activities within it, the study cannot succeed. (p. 56)

Accessibility concerns geographic location and ability to gain entry and cooperation from pertinent "gatekeepers." The term *ideal* again comes into the picture. Many of the same considerations previously discussed in selecting a research topic, such as personal capabilities and feasibility factors (e.g., finances, transportation, family, lodging, food costs, and equipment), apply in selecting a suitable site.

Gaining entry into a possible site is an endeavor that must be well planned and included in the site-selection process. The keys to access any setting are in the hands of certain gatekeepers, or those who have the authority to allow one to enter their world. In speaking with these people one must remember that naturalistic inquiry is highly interactive, depending on persistent observations, intense focused conversations and interviews, and the collection of volumes of documents. Rapport, trust, congeniality, and other aspects of interpersonal relationships between researcher and respondents is an ongoing process that begins with the initial contact with the gatekeeper(s). Marshall and Rossman (1989) write:

> Researchers who conduct qualitative research will need to propose and develop roles that ease entry, facilitate receptivity of environments and participants' cooperation. They will need to demonstrate that they can conduct research in such a way that neither the setting nor the people in it are harmed. (p. 63)

Gaining access to a suitable site can be very difficult and may force the researcher to change the focus of the study. Taylor (1992) originally proposed to study the power associations of addicts in bureaucratic organizations. She had identified several groups of addicts who had agreed to be subjects in her study and had received informal encouragement from several business organizations that she considered as sites. However, these plans were thwarted when the encouragement she had received earlier evaporated at each proposed site as insurmountable barriers were quietly but systematically raised. Taylor had never satisfactorily gained the support of the gatekeepers, primarily because their control of their organizations was threatened by her proposed research and because they consequently used that control to exclude her. The chronicle of her foiled attempts to implement this study eventually resulted in another study (Taylor, 1992) that analyzed the problem of negotiating access to organizations. This analysis identifies some of the underlying problems in gaining access to a proposed research site and also identifies possible strategies for overcoming these problems. This study is highly recommended for anyone who is in the process of identifying a site for a naturalistic study.

Yeager and Kram (1990), in their study of corporate ethics, contacted 12 corporations—5 banks and 7 high-technology companies—before they were able to secure two research sites. Although, as in Taylor's case, several of the companies showed initial interest, they declined to participate after learning of the details of the proposed research. Although the reasons given for declining were often vague, the researchers assumed that they were generally related to the study's intrusiveness (management time, data sensitivity), to relatively low interest in the ethical domain, or to a combination of the two reasons. After gaining access to the two sites, they took steps to develop liaison relationships with internal groups of managers in both sites. These liaison groups developed internal support for the project and a wider base of project legitimacy. They also helped in establishing relationships with interviewees and, though they were not asked to be interviewees themselves, proved to be important sources of data. Yeager and Kram also enhanced their relationships with managers and executives in the two sites by promising them copies of the final feedback report, soliciting their responses to the report, and asking them for changes, corroboration, and additional information that would enhance the analysis and the practical utility of the research.

The researcher must also determine for a potential site if there is a high probability that there is a rich mix of many of the processes, people, programs, and interactions that may be part of the research problem (Marshall & Rossman, 1989). This can be accomplished through "prior ethnography," that is, visiting the site and conversing with respondents, observing, recording, and discerning if the site "fits" the research objectives.

Lincoln and Guba (1985) write:

> Such prior ethnography not only helps to diminish the obtrusiveness of the investigator but also provides a baseline of cultural accommodation and informational orientation that will be invaluable in increasing both the effectiveness and the efficiency of the formal work. It prepares the inquirer's mind for what will come later and so serves to sensitize and hone the human instrument. (p. 251)

In her study of elementary school principals, Bifano (1987) selected three sites for extensive study. In the prior ethnography stage of study at one of the sites, the researcher determined that the site did not have the characteristics she wished to study. She also found in her prior ethnography at this site that she was being denied access to important sources of data. Consequently, she abandoned the site and selected an alternative site. Regardless of how perfect the site may seem for answering the research questions, the researcher must have access to the means of addressing the research questions. Bifano could have continued with the selected site and found partial answers to her research question, but those answers could not be considered to represent an accurate, complete picture of the school under study. The researcher must avoid the temptation to compromise the quality of his or her research for the sake of convenience.

A decision the researcher will need to make is whether to conduct his or her study at one site or in multiple sites. One thing that makes this a difficult decision is the preconditioning of years of traditional research assumptions and methodology. Generally speaking, the notion has been to define the target population and then randomly draw a representative sample from the population. In some cases a small sample size would be appropriate, and in others a large sample size would be better, but it is virtually unheard of to have a sample size of one. However, we must remember that the overall purpose of generalizability in conventional research is not present in naturalistic research.

A caveat is not to rush into a commitment to a single setting for inquiry until ample pre-ethnography and investigation are conducted. A potential problem of reducing the investigation to one setting is that a case may later turn out not to be the case it was thought to be at the outset. Thus, single-case designs require careful examination of the potential site to minimize the chances of misrepresentation and to maximize the access needed to collect the case study evidence (Yin, 1984).

There are some cases when several sites may be preferred. For example, if a group of researchers is studying a particular problem, several sites could be identified and the researchers could individually investigate single sites and then convene to analyze their findings. Other times, an individual may desire to study two or more divergent sites to test the transferability of constructed realities from one site to the other. The decision on the number of sites should not be determined by preconceived notions or pressures from traditional researchers but by the research problem and the purpose of the study. For many purposes one site will be sufficient.

Another consideration that is involved at the point of site selection is planning for the proper amount of time for the researcher to spend at the site. All naturalistic researchers are faced with the dilemma of either spending long (a month to a year or more) or short (five days to a few weeks) periods of time at a setting. During long periods of time, the researcher has more opportunities for personal interaction, gathering greater amounts of data and constructing shared realities with persons in the setting being studied. However, the disadvantage includes the danger of the researcher over-identifying with the respondents and thereby destroying the value that can be brought to shared constructions by an outside observer. There are possible disadvantages of a short-term visit as well. For example, a brief stay might prohibit the amount of time needed to build rapport, develop trust, understand the culture, and obtain a sufficient amount of in-depth data, thereby diminishing the probability of constructing shared realities with persons in the setting. So how long is long enough? The answer to that question is relative to the research problem, to the context's scope and complexity, and to the researcher's abilities and skills.

Working Hypotheses

Implicit in the process of formulating the research problem, focusing questions, and designating an appropriate site(s) is the evolution of working hypotheses. In fact, whether stated or not, working hypotheses exist in seminal form before the research process begins and continue to take shape through the completion of the study. Before research begins, these hypotheses are embedded in the value orientation of the researcher and are based on her or his preconceived notions about the topic and reasons for the study. As the researcher moves through the research process these notions should be explicated and continuously refined. In some cases the working hypotheses can change to such an extent that they have no resemblance to their original forms. However, these hypotheses should not be viewed as a priori null hypotheses that appear in conventional research and are designed to be accepted or rejected.

An example of the evolution of a tentative working hypothesis can be seen in a study of a shopping mall conducted by several of the authors. A general guiding notion going into the study was stated as such: "The shopping mall is an appropriate representation of American society in the last quarter of the 20th century." As the study proceeded and took form, the essence of the tentative statement became increasingly metaphorical. The statement was never regarded as a generalizable postulate to be accepted or rejected, but rather as a proposition to be altered to portray the particular context. This approach allowed the inquirers to retain the flexibility needed to allow the focus of the research to evolve during the process itself. Some of the evolutionary developments of the original statement can be seen below:

> Certain aspects of the shopping mall depict American society in the last quarter of the twentieth century.
>
> The shopping mall is an appropriate representation of only certain segments of American society.
>
> The shopping mall depicts the cultural pluralism of American society in the last quarter of the twentieth century.
>
> The shopping mall is the modern translation of yesterday's village square.

The working hypothesis as it was originally stated and in its final form was always considered transient and tentative for both the situation under investigation as well as for other situations. Lincoln and Guba (1985) give insight into this conception:

> [T]here are always differences in context from situation to situation, and even the single situation differs over time. It is said that a Chinese philosopher, upon being asked whether it is possible to cross the same river twice, replied that it is not possible to cross the same river even once! Constant flux militates against conclusions that are always and forever true; they can

only be said to be true under such and such conditions and circumstances.
(p. 124)

In essence, working hypotheses are general statements applicable to the specific context under investigation. These formulations give meaning and direction to the research. They are tools used to give guidance to the project and should be progressively modified and refined as patterns of phenomena emerge.

Working hypotheses are also bridges between studies. A thorough, naturalistic study of high school A provides many insights and understandings about that organization. These insights and understandings are not generalizable to high school B; but, having conducted the study of high school A, or read a thick description of the A context by another person, the researcher should be better prepared to conduct a study of high school B. Why? Because the experience with A, whether firsthand or vicarious, will have enabled the researcher to formulate working hypotheses that can be modified and refined to give insights into the new context. In a similar manner, working hypotheses can connect separate studies of the same setting. For Boelen (1992), working hypotheses were generated, modified, and refined as Whyte's constructions and conclusions first interacted with her own questions about his work and then with the data she collected from interviews with the residents of "Cornerville."

The testable, working hypotheses of naturalistic research, like the hypotheses of more conventional research, give direction to the research and to the researcher. Unlike traditional hypotheses, though, they genuinely interact with data collection and analysis, modifying and being modified as the research process continues.

Getting Started: An Interactive Process

It should be remembered that when a researcher embarks on a study, the process is seldom a straightforward one. The steps of formulating the research problem and questions, site selection, and the generation of working hypotheses are more likely to be interactive than discrete. Two examples will help to clarify this.

A graduate student was seeking to identify a problem for a dissertation (Jackson, 1991). For some time he had been very interested in the habits and perceptions of older workers but had not refined his area of interest beyond that point. Near the end of his formal coursework he became engaged in an internship in a university's physical plant department. During this experience he learned that the department really wanted to learn more about the operation of its custodial and landscape services. Because many of the employees in these areas were older, the researcher linked the problem roughly formulated by the physical plant department with his own research interest to develop the idea for a naturalistic study that would focus on custodial and landscape workers who were 50 years of age and older. This merger took shape in the following general statement of a research problem.

> The training literature contains numerous anecdotal and descriptive accounts of training older workers, but only limited and fragmentary research findings specifically related to the training of older adults. The literature contains even less concerning the training of older workers who perform low level technology jobs. Consequently, there is a need for a research-based comprehensive model to facilitate the effective training and support needs of older adults to cope with the challenges they will encounter during the 1990-2000 time period. This is specifically true for those employed in the lower technology areas of custodial and landscape maintenance workers. (Jackson, 1991, p. 3)

This in turn led to the following research objectives:

1. Determine the training and support needs of older custodial and landscape workers at the university.
2. Develop a model which will facilitate the training and support of those older workers. (p. 5)

The researcher started with several implicit working hypotheses that guided him in the formulation of the interview questions that he used to gather data from the workers:

> Older workers can continue to be productive in most of their jobs.
> Older workers can continue to be trained, given the right strategies for training them.
> Longer utilization of older workers has both positive and negative aspects.
> Older workers, even in lower level technology jobs, can be significant partners in their own retraining. (Jackson, 1992)

Notice that a natural flow between the various elements that we have identified is important in initiating a study. This flow will be different for every study, but there are several things the researcher can do to facilitate it. Although the flow was "natural" in this case, it did not simply happen. It happened because the researcher had an identified interest and considerable background in it. He also consciously put himself in situations (i.e., the internship) that involved older workers and offered the possibility of an emergent topic.

Notice also how the study emerged as an implicit contract that served both the needs of the institution (i.e., the need to learn about their custodial and landscape services) and the needs of the researcher (i.e., the desire to find a dissertation that focused on older workers). This is ideal for a naturalistic study. The study is not done to someone, but rather emerges as a mutually beneficial relationship between researcher, institution, and respondents.

Mobley (1992) had been in the field of nutrition education for 25 years when she began her doctoral research. Over this time she had grown increasingly concerned about professional interaction with clients and the impact of this interaction on the changed behavior of the clients. Because poor nutrition patterns are highly correlated with low income and low literacy and also with minority ethnicity, an underlying question that emerged in her mind was: "How do we propose interventions that will make observable differences in the nutrition habits of people in these at-risk groups?" Because, through her professional contacts, she knew people in the field of diabetes education and because she had access to diabetes education classes that served a low-income, predominantly minority population, she brought her interest and opportunity together in this problem statement:

> Diabetes education designed to meet the needs of low-income minorities has been delivered through media programs and the design and production of teaching materials. Additionally, attempts to increase public awareness of the relationship between obesity and the incidence of diabetes have been supported through screening programs. Much of the research on education of diabetics has focused on whether patient education contributes to metabolic control. Yet, there is a need to gain insight into the motives, fears, and desires of patients who are required to participate in educational programs and to identify effective application of educational principles to diabetes education. . . . Educational programs have been predicated on perceived needs and theoretical models that may not address the needs or attitudes of lower socioeconomic groups. Educational needs have been defined by those who deliver education, not by those who are required to participate in diabetes education programs designed to improve self-care management of a disease. (Mobley, 1991, p. 3)

Note that several working hypotheses are implicitly or explicitly advanced in this statement of the problem:

> Diabetics from low-income minority groups have motives, fears, and desires that are different from other diabetics.
>
> Perceived needs of diabetics and existing theoretical models may not address the needs of diabetics from lower social economic groups.
>
> There is a difference between what those who deliver a diabetes education program intend to happen, what those who participate in it perceive as happening, and what actually happens.

These working hypotheses led in turn to the following research questions that then led Mobley into her study:

1. What is happening in the Diabetes Complications Intervention Grant Education Program?
2. How do the clients/patients participating in the diabetes education program perceive what is happening?
3. What do the clients/patients want to happen in the program to assist in the self-care management of their disease and, more specifically, the management of their nutritional status? (Mobley, 1991, p. 4)

Conclusion

Seasoned mountaineers know the importance of carefully and methodically putting one foot in front of the other, of taking one conscious step at a time when ascending precipitous peaks. To look beyond the next step would not only put them in danger, but also might cause them to be so overwhelmed that they would discontinue their climb. In the Everest-like task of writing a dissertation or conducting any significant study, it is important to give much attention to the initial steps of identifying a researchable problem of genuine interest, carefully developing the research problem and phrasing the research questions, and identifying the best site within the inquirer's resources. This will not only increase the probability of the project's completion, but also help to ensure the study's success.

For Further Study

1. Compare and contrast the alternative ways in which Whyte (1943) and Agee and Evans (1988) became involved in their respective studies. Or, if you prefer, select two other major studies for this comparison and contrast.

2. Read Hollingshead (1975). What is the focus of the study as Hollingshead perceived it? How does this compare with the way that the people of Elmtown perceived it? What implications does this have for naturalistic researchers?

3. Think about the focus of the naturalistic study you began in Chapter 1. What steps can you take at this point to refine that focus? Take those steps.

4

Designing a Naturalistic Inquiry

GIVEN THE NATURALISTIC researcher's insistence on remaining true to the context, one may ask, "Should there even be research design in a naturalistic study?" The answer to that important question is, "Yes—to some extent." Design in a naturalistic study takes great care to see that it is not imposed arbitrarily on the context and that it takes into consideration the full richness of the context. As a result, the design of a naturalistic study is usually not fully established before the study begins but emerges as data are collected, preliminary analysis is conducted, and the context becomes more fully described.

Consider the key components of traditional design (Krathwohl, 1985):

1. conclusions from prior research
2. theoretical perspective
3. research questions and hypotheses
4. methodological design
5. data collection
6. data analysis (descriptive statistics)
7. significance of the results (inferential statistics)
8. conclusions

Although there are aspects of most of these components in naturalistic research design, it would be inappropriate to think that one could make the same a priori plans for a naturalistic research project as one might make for a conventional project. The primary difference lies in the specificity of the original research plan. The naturalistic researcher should consider insights gained from previous studies. In fact, the naturalistic researcher may even utilize a theoretical perspective if that perspective was grounded in prior naturalistic research (Lincoln & Guba, 1985). The naturalistic researcher will have research questions (but not definitive hypotheses). The naturalistic researcher will need to have general plans for at least preliminary methods of gathering data, but these plans will be much less definitively formed than in a conventional study. The naturalistic researcher will need to consider how data will be analyzed after they have been gathered in order to make certain that he or she collects data in such a way that they are usable. The naturalistic researcher will need to give thought to the meaning of his or her study while keeping in mind that transferability rests with the receiving context (Lincoln & Guba, 1985; Guba & Lincoln, 1989).

Designing a Naturalistic Study

Lincoln and Guba (1985, p. 226) provide a practical definition of design in the naturalistic paradigm. They state that design "means planning for certain broad contingencies without, however, indicating exactly what will be done in relation to each." Whereas the conventional researcher is required to make a priori decisions as to how he or she will deal with particular variables and occurrences, the naturalistic researcher "as one committed to the primacy of natural context" can make no such decisions. The naturalistic researcher will need to plan for anticipated circumstances, but decisions as to how one will deal with them must be left until the context of time, place, and human interactions is better understood.

In Chapter 3 we dealt with how one gets started on the study. Having gotten this far, what does the naturalistic researcher need to do next? It is at this point that many beginning researchers feel some uncertainty because the emergent nature of naturalistic inquiry precludes the researcher from many of the conventional design techniques and securities. However, while this may be viewed as a handicap, the naturalistic paradigm offers direction and advantages that the conventional paradigm simply cannot match. We shall try to illustrate why this is the case.

Conventional research in social contexts has been patterned after the methods used in the physical sciences; but the physical sciences are very different in important ways. Conventional research, as we have noted, makes every attempt to separate the inquirer from the object of inquiry so that the research will not be contaminated. We will not here try to dispute the advantages that such a stance has for the study of atoms or rabbits. However, there are important differences between such studies and the study of social contexts. The researcher cannot get inside the atom; he or she can only "see" (i.e. , make inferences and deduce knowledge about) them from the outside. The researcher cannot go and live among the rabbits or communicate and share constructed realities with them. Yet for the naturalistic researcher, the ability to get inside the social context, to share constructed realities with the stakeholders in that context, and to construct new realities that enhance both the knowledge of the researcher and the knowledge and efficacy of the stakeholders is the essence of research. Research design must take these factors into consideration. This in turn means that naturalistic research design remains tentative until it is implemented. Even after the research has been initiated, the shape of subsequent phases of research will still be refined as additional information is learned from the social context itself.

Conventional research design is based on what might be considered "black box" research. The researcher specifies in advance what instrumentation will be used, at what points, and with whom (usually selected randomly because the opportunity to distinguish among quality of respondents has been denied as a self-imposed restriction). Similar restrictions are put on the output of the research (i.e., what will be admitted as valid evidence and the manner in which it will be classified).

Building on this same metaphor, the naturalistic researcher climbs inside the "black box" (and finds, to the surprise of traditional research colleagues, that there is light inside of it). There he or she can distinguish among stakeholders, determine how they are related, and choose among respondents for qualities related to the research. The researcher can also test other information (his or her own constructions as well as data in documents and records) against the constructions of the stakeholders and bring their separate constructions into contact with each other, so that they can be mutually understood and expanded and so that shared constructions and empowerment can be developed. As the researcher operates within the social context (the black box), he or she will move around the circle of stakeholders many times, sharing constructions and building common understanding and direction. From this process, the final shape of the study and the form in which it will be reported gradually emerge. Allowing for this emerging process is fundamental to naturalistic design.

There are, however, several things that the naturalistic researcher can plan in advance to facilitate this emergent process. We may consider each of these briefly.

1. *Negotiating and developing the conditions of entry.* In Chapter 3 we talked about the importance of site selection in getting started on a naturalistic study. We also briefly discussed the importance of establishing the conditions of entry. We will discuss this further in a subsequent section of this chapter. To this we would also add the equally important need for continuing to reestablish and develop the agreement on which the research is pursued. We will note in Chapter 7 that conditions of entry can never really be finalized with the gatekeepers to a social context before the study starts; they must be renegotiated as the study progresses. Plans for the renegotiation process should be built into the early plans of the researcher.

2. *Planning for purposive sample selection.* The researcher must consider early how members of different stakeholding groups will be selected as initial respondents in the study. This will be discussed further in Chapter 5.

3. *Planning for data collection.* Similarly, the researcher needs to begin clarifying what data he or she will seek from the social context and what strategies (combinations of interviews, observations, and document search) he or she initially believes are likely to find the desired data. Clarifying these data and strategies will be further developed in Chapter 5.

4. *Planning for data analysis.* In the same way, even before he or she formally starts on the study, the researcher can begin to envision how continuing analysis will interact with the data collected and how a final analysis will be conducted prior to generating a report of the study.

5. *Planning for quality in the study.* In addition to planning to establish trustworthiness through the way the study is conducted, the researcher will consider ways that authenticity (discussed in Chapter 7) will be built into the study.

6. *Planning for dissemination of the study's findings.* The researcher needs to consider who the audiences are for the final report of the study, the purpose of communicating to those audiences, and the mode that will most effectively communicate to them.

7. *Developing a logistical plan for the study.* The researcher needs to consider how long the study is likely to take, how the various places of the study can be scheduled, and how the study will be supported.

8. *Reviewing the tentative design.* The researcher needs to regularly reexamine the provisions he or she has made in each of the above steps

Table 4.1   Scheduled Phases of a High School Case Study

PHASE I	PHASE II
Begin a daily or weekly journal	Continue journal
Conduct prior ethnography	Conduct peer debriefing sessions
Determine interview questions for unstructured, exploratory interviews	Modify grounded theories
	Determine interview questions for structured interviews
Conduct unstructured interviews and unitize data	Conduct structured interviews and unitize data
Collect critical incidents	
Begin member-checking process	Continue member-checking process
Examine referential materials and artifacts	Continue collecting critical incidents
	Continue analyzing referential materials and artifacts
Begin data analysis (categorizing data)	Continue data analysis
Conduct negative case analysis	
Develop preliminary grounded theories	
PHASE III	**PHASE IV**
Continue journal	Carry out a comprehensive member check (review panel)
Conduct peer debriefing sessions	Revise case study
Modify grounded theories	Commission and facilitate the external audit
Continue member-checking process	
Develop provisional outline	Exit the school
Write provisional case study	Release the report
Conduct member checks	
Revise case study	

Excerpted from Skipper, 1989.

in the tentative design. New information and new conditions raise new questions that require the researcher to change plans and strategies.

The scheduled sequence of a study conducted by one of the authors is shown in Table 4.1.

As the researcher climbs into the black box, these elements serve as an initial road map; they are, in fact, part of his or her design to respond to the research problem and research questions that have been formulated. The definition of this problem, the questions that have been formulated to pursue it, and the working hypotheses that have emanated from it are constantly refined and expanded as this design process is implemented. We cannot emphasize enough that there is a continuing interactive process (to which we will regularly refer) as the design is implemented. This interactive, circular process of data collection, data analysis, and design review continues until a point of redundancy is reached where no significant new information emerges or no major new constructions are being developed. Although there will never be a complete end to the emergence of new information or new constructions of reality, redundancy may be considered to have occurred when efforts necessary to gather new information "cannot be justified in terms of the additional outlay of energy and resources" (Lincoln & Guba, 1985, p. 233).

Conditions of Entry

As we noted in Chapter 3, gaining entry to a research site is an important element in initiating the study. The conditions of entry, as they are negotiated, become important elements of the research design. They set the limits for many of the subsequent decisions that the researcher will make.

According to Johnson (1975), the nature of the problem faced in gaining entry depends on whether the field researcher chooses to study a large-scale, formal organization, such as a welfare office, or an open setting, such as a street-corner gang. In addition, the nature of the problem depends on whether the researcher proposes to do overt or covert research. A decision to conduct a secret investigation in which the researcher does not make known what he is doing solves the problem of gaining entry, but such a decision does not guarantee that the members of the setting will trust the researcher and allow him or her access to valid information.

In a study of a maximum security prison the researcher learned that to gain entry to the prison he would have to be an employee. As a result, he went through the complete correctional officer training and became a prison guard. His training protected his safety and the safety of others while he worked in the prison. In the beginning only a few individuals in the entire system knew of his research purpose. The advantage was that it kept him from being inundated with people with "axes to grind" (Fleisher, 1989, p. 93). The disadvantage was that in the eyes of the prisoners, "When you carry them keys on your hip, I don't care who . . . you say you are, you're one of them" (Fleisher, 1989, pp. 97-98).

In sociology it is more likely that the research settings will not be covert studies in a formally organized bureaucracy or business corporation; they are more likely to be overt studies in such settings as a street-corner gang or ethnic community. Some examples are Whyte's *Street Corner Society* (1943), Gans's *The Urban Villagers* (1982) and *The Levittowners* (1967), and Gallaher's *Plainville Fifteen Years Later* (1961). This type of research appears to differ from research in large-scale organizations because successful entry for the researcher is much more dependent on the field researcher's ability to establish a rapport with a key leader in the community. This key leader will often shoulder much of the responsibility of seeing that others understand and accept the research project. The accomplishment of successful entry also partially revolves around the field researcher's ability to explain his interests in terms that make sense to the members of the setting. In other words, the members want to know what the researcher is up to and a plausible rationale that justifies the operation. In other words, "What's in it for me?" or "Why should I bother talk to you?" Appropriate answers to these questions will allow the researcher and respondent to make an exchange, consciously or unconsciously, giving each other what they both desire or need.

According to Johnson (1975), however, this exchange model of interaction is an oversimplification of the process because it overlooks the importance of existing relationships of power in the context. For example, it overlooks that some will respond simply because higher-ups have approved the research. Others will respond to relieve boredom or loneliness. Some will respond as an opportunity to express grievances. The researcher must be aware that there are many possible motivations to respond.

Some researchers use a three-stage progressive-entry strategy (Johnson, 1975). For example, in a study of a welfare office the researcher asked for permission to interview her colleagues during their off-duty hours as an aid to a larger research project in social welfare. The second stage was a request to observe and accompany social workers during their everyday activities. The third stage was a request for permission to use a tape recorder. These stages were made by "walking through" the requests. In other words, the requests were made and granted in face-to-face interactions. The reason for this process was that the researcher was concerned that the request for the use of tape recorder would be threatening and perhaps denied. By using this process, the research project would not completely die if this one request were denied.

Another strategy (Johnson, 1975) to aid gaining entry is to have a letter of introduction from either administrative officials in the organization, letters from university officials on letterhead, or both. Such letters persuade officials to grant clearance to research by lending bureaucratic approval or academic respectability to the researcher. Experience has also shown that the letter should be as open-ended as possible rather than a longer, more detailed proposal that could provide ammunition for any member of the organization who might choose to invoke organizational rules to reject it. Also, the researcher does not want to lock the study into a path that may be contrary to the design of the study as it emerges during data collection and analysis.

In making decisions about gaining entry one point cannot be overemphasized: Successful entry is not the beginning of a research project but rather follows after the investigator collects background information concerning how things typically work in a given setting.

Emergent Design

The design of a study is the attempt of a researcher to give order to some set of phenomena so that they will make sense to the researcher and so that the researcher can communicate that sense to others. The conventional researcher can usually decide after a fairly short time what variation of some conventional design or combination of designs ought to be applied in a given situation; the decision is usually made prior to the collection of data about the phenomena being studied. The naturalistic researcher, however, recognizing the complexity of any human setting, goes into the setting with only as much design as he or she believes is faithful to the context and will help to answer questions about it. Like the descriptive linguist learning a new language from native speakers, the naturalistic researcher recognizes the complexity of the context and allows structure to build only as his or her understanding of that context and of the respondents' constructions of reality allows the design to emerge.

By the time the researcher finds a rough focus for the study and begins looking for a site, a design is beginning to emerge. By the time a site has been identified and arrangements have been made to work in it, a considerable amount of design is already in place. At this point the design is still open to change, and the naturalistic researcher will continue to look for ways to improve it even after the study has formally begun; but some important decisions will have been made. Two examples will help to illustrate this.

Recall our example from Chapter 1 that related how one of the authors, as a member of a team of consultants, took on the task of evaluating the educational program of a large state institution. The reader will recall that the task of the team was no more specific than this; within this overall task, the author's charge was to provide an organizational analysis of the institution. As was noted earlier, the charge was indeed a nebulous one, and the team had to move ahead with the study very much on its own and to design the study as its understanding of the institution grew. However, even at that time the author had considerable structure and was beginning to design his portion of the study even as he accepted the invitation to join the team. Although he had never worked in or studied an institution like this one before, it was a public institution and he had spent considerable time in public schools and universities, both as a participant and as a researcher. Further, he was asked to provide an organizational analysis, and this is what he usually did for schools and other educational organizations. Already he had some ideas about what he was looking for in this institution and a variety of ideas about how he might obtain that information. Furthermore, as a member of a team, he had agreed to meet periodically with the other team members and to provide a report that would be a compatible piece of the overall evaluation. These requirements put constraints on what he would do and how he would do it. In addition, although the institution that commissioned the evaluation gave no specific direction or restriction on how the evaluation would be done, it did request that the final report be ready in three months' time. Given the background and expectations of the researcher and the constraints imposed by the team and the employing institution, a large number of design alternatives had been eliminated.

Four years earlier the same author had been asked by the principal of a new inner-city high school to work with him as he opened the school and as the first faculty and students were brought into it. The principal and the author (at that time a professor in a local college) agreed in general terms that the author would have open access to everything that occurred in the school—individual faculty, individual students, classes, meetings, school activities, and so on. In addition, it was agreed that the author would be given ready access to all the school's public documents and would attend certain functions, such as the principal's cabinet meetings, whenever his schedule allowed it. It was also agreed that the author would give the principal feedback on what was happening in the school and suggestions for how its operation could be strengthened, without revealing confidential information or the identities of individuals when doing so would cast them in a negative light. In return, the author was free to collect data on the school and to analyze and use them for his own research. The initial agreement was no more specific than this, and at the time it was made, probably neither principal nor professor was absolutely sure what would come of it. However, it was a beginning, and as the author began to consider its implications for his research, a design was starting to emerge. He had done studies of other high schools, including two others in the very same city. As a result, even during his initial talk with the principal, ideas were already running through his mind about how he would develop a purposive sample of interviews and organizations. Because he planned at that point to spend one academic year in the school and knew that he could spend approximately two days a week on campus, he began to develop a rough schedule for data collection and interim reports. Initial questions to guide him were already forming in his mind. The design for his study was taking shape, and although many unanticipated events would change its course during the year, several key guidelines for the study were determined during that first conversation with the principal.

Once the study is begun, the design of a naturalistic study continues to emerge. As the researcher gets deeper and deeper into the context, he or she will see that early questions and working hypotheses, however helpful in getting started, are very simplistic. First sources of data reveal others that the researcher could not have imagined. Regularities, assumed for an organization because they were present in similar organizations, are not present. Unanticipated patterns and events require the researcher to think and perceive in completely new ways. The beginning naturalistic researcher, looking back at the original tentative design for the study, may even suppose that, because in retrospect it appears so naive, it was a useless venture. However, those early naive questions and that tentative, simplistic early design, in fact, often pave the way for a rich study, and they serve as a useful benchmark to remind the naturalistic researcher how much progress has been made as the context for the study is more fully understood.

In the case of our first example, in which this author was a member of an evaluation team, the researcher made several major changes in his original design once he began interacting with respondents in the institution. As was his customary manner in conducting an organizational analysis, he asked each unit in the institution to furnish him with role descriptions and its organizational chart. His purpose in so doing was to obtain a map that would help him select a sample for interviews and observations and to formulate items for interview questions and observation schedules. The director of one unit called the author one morning at his office to indicate that his unit had a problem and asked him if he could spend two hours with him and his staff that afternoon. The meeting began by the unit's staff confessing that they really did not have an organizational chart or role descriptions, at least not in the conventional sense, and they were not sure how to construct them. They had requested the meeting to obtain the author's help in overcoming that obstacle. What the author discovered was that, although the staff had never specifically planned it, the operational structure of the unit was nearly a textbook representation of Rensis Likert's System 4 (Likert, 1967), an organization in which role responsibilities overlap in a mutually supportive fashion that empowers individuals as they collaboratively accomplish the organization's mission. Although loudly acclaimed by many organizational theorists and observers, that type of organization is still uncommon. The traditional organizational chart and role descriptions do not fit it very well. This discovery produced major shifts in the author's way of perceiving the institution, including the way in which the separate units were structured as well as how they related to their clients, to the central administration, and to one another. New questions for all units were produced. A richer basis for comparisons and contrasts among them and more productive ways for evaluating them emerged. In many ways, that simple discovery completely changed the nature of the author's design. Unquestionably, the information provided in that two-hour meeting would have emerged as the author studied the unit in depth, but coming relatively early in the study, it provided an efficiency for the major part of the study that would not have been possible without it. A tight initial design that was not allowed to make full use of this new information when it emerged would have prevented it from making the major contribution to the study that it did.

The author's research design in the large city high school was modified in a similar way. Though he had spent time in scores of high schools and completed studies of several of them, he found that this particular high school was truly unique in ways that he could not have anticipated from studying its demographic data or its formal organizational structure. The unique interactions among staff members, with community members, and between the principal and all parties created a unique culture for this school that separated it from all others. Crises arose and helped define this culture as it was emerging, not only for the researcher but also for all of the organization's participants. Some crises served to reinforce what the author had already learned about the culture. Some, however, served to completely rearrange his existing understanding of the culture and directed him to reformulate questions and redirect his data collection plans in ways that he had never anticipated. The principal and faculty, who were learning the culture while they helped to create it, served as eager collaborators with the author as the research design emerged. "Have you thought about it this way?" "Do you think that what we're doing is really different from what other high schools do?" Such questions forced the author to continually refine his premises, and as he did so, both his understanding of the school and his design for data collection and analysis became more precise.

Dingwall, Eekelaar, and Murray (1983), in their study of child abuse in Great Britain, found a similar need to shift elements of their design after it was in progress. After compiling 27 case files, attending 11 full hearings and 25 case conferences, and conducting 17 interviews, they discovered their procedures were not telling them everything they needed. They determined that a filtering process was operating that "resulted in the apparent irrelevance of conferences as arenas for [decision making] as opposed to establishing a commitment to some action effectively decided upon in advance" (p. 27). They decided, therefore, to switch their focus to the internal operations of the health and personal social services. This shift in procedures led to observation and analysis of the "successive sifting of candidate cases by fieldworkers, by their supervisors, by those making and by those receiving referrals, which led to the identification of children as having been abused or neglected and their allocation between the various disposal options available" (p. 27).

Even after all the major pieces of the design are in place (research questions, interview formats, observation schedules, and time lines) there is always the need for fine tuning. After considerable preliminary work, Allen (1990) posited the following interview questions:

1. How would you describe this high school?
2. How would you describe the administration?
3. How would you describe the principal's style?
4. How are decisions made here?
5. What effect do you see the principal's job having on other people getting their jobs done (students as learners, teachers as instructors, and so on)?
6. How would you describe faculty and staff morale?
7. What problems do you see at this high school?
8. What else should I know about to get an accurate picture of the school?
9. In order to gain a clear understanding of the high school, I need to get as many different viewpoints as possible. Please look over this list of names of people I have interviewed. Who has a perspective other than what you would think I have been given by those on this list?

Responses in his early interviews, however, led him to add two more questions:

10. With the morale question, we were looking primarily at the faculty and staff. Let us add the students to that. How would you describe the climate of the school?

11. What professional affiliations do you have?

After lengthy data collection, Question 11 was found to provide no pertinent information and was subsequently dropped. That determination was carefully made by analyzing the content of the responses and looking for possible relationships between them and other information provided. Answers to that question were consistently close-ended (such as "Texas State Teachers Association" or "American Federation of Teachers") and did not appear related to the type of information provided in response to other questions. The other questions all provided significant amounts of information relevant to the research questions. They also occasionally provided information that, while interesting, had no relevance to the study. For example, as part of her response to the question about morale, one teacher commented, "Not having a phone in the departmental office makes it difficult for me to call parents when a student is absent or misbehaves." While that comment should be considered as relevant to that teacher's state of mind, it may have little significance to the overall morale of the faculty and staff at the school. It is incumbent on the researcher to consider all information as it is gathered. Information may later be considered to be of so little significance that its inclusion does not further thicken the description of the setting. If the inconvenience of not having a phone had been reported by several sources or if this inconvenience appeared to be related to parallel concerns of other faculty, it would have been given further consideration as likely having a bearing on the morale of the faculty and, consequently, on the overall culture of the school. Given that a comment may initially appear to be irrelevant and later be found to be quite relevant, it is best to err on the side of overinclusion until the data have been analyzed.

Summary

These elements of a research design for a naturalistic study are both more complex and more flexible than those of a conventional research design. Like language they are attempts to classify and order the activity of the researcher so that the human mind can appropriately relate to new experiences as they are encountered. Unlike the design of conventional research, however, they constitute a "language" that adapts rapidly as experience shifts and new experience is encountered. The complexity of a naturalistic design is impossible to predict with any precision; it can best be described by tracing its evolution in the researcher's log after the study has been completed. The best advice to the beginning naturalistic researcher is to "plan to be flexible." The preliminary plans that constitute the elements of a naturalistic design, as we have outlined them, will often be difficult to separate from each other in practice. They will blend together and shift as the research design continues to unfold. Because the human mind needs a language in order to project itself into new arenas, we believe that the elements we have outlined will be helpful to the new researcher. However, the researcher must use them to nurture the emerging design, not to dictate the details of its implementation. The ability to handle complexity with flexibility will be a major factor in the success of the naturalistic researcher.

For Further Study

1. Review one or more of the following: Whyte (1943), Wolcott (1973), Hollingshead (1975), Lightfoot (1983), Agee and Evans (1988), or a major sociological or anthropological study of your choice. Infer the design that the authors had in their minds at the beginning of their works. Outline the inferred design for one of these studies.

2. Develop an initial design for the naturalistic study you began in Chapter 1. This design should be sufficient to satisfy the persons for whom you are conducting the study. If possible, obtain feedback in writing from these persons. Write a written response to this feedback.

5

Gathering Data

A NEWBORN HAS an amazing capacity for gathering and analyzing an array of data. He or she comes into the world knowing virtually nothing and is bombarded by tastes, smells, sights, and sounds. Conclusions emerge as he or she begins to understand and relate to the immediate world. For instance, a smile or chuckle is an appropriate response to an adult making an absurd face or repeating nonsensical phrases. A cry will get dinner or a diaper change. As time goes on, the young child begins to use language to classify the unstructured experiences that surround him or her. Words, phrases, and gestures help in communicating with others and in reinforcing the conclusions drawn about the environment.

This natural inductive analysis—or constructing meaning from a multitude of heterogeneous, specific data—is often stifled in the formal educational process and must be relearned for most adults. The educational systems many times replace discovery learning with deductive and didactic approaches, and by the time a person is in graduate school he or she must regain what originally came naturally. In this chapter we will consider how the naturalistic researcher seeks and collects data about human activity that will enable him or her to break the barriers of separate constructed realities.

The Purpose of Gathering Data

The primary purpose of gathering data in naturalistic inquiry is to gain the ability to construct reality in ways that are consistent and compatible with the constructions of a setting's inhabitants. This requires that the naturalistic researcher be able to experience what the "natives" experience and to see that experience in the way that they see it. A common language (such as English) facilitates the researcher's entry into the setting and facilitates the collection of data, but beyond this entry level the same "common" language often inhibits the flow of meaning because it is used to mask differences in the constructed realities of researcher and respondent. Now, because it is primarily the researcher who is trying to enhance the flow of meaning, it is the researcher who will have to take overt measures to overcome the barriers. The respondent will generally not be conscious that dictionary meanings of words do not necessarily lead to the researcher's faithful reconstructions of the respondent's reality. Nor is it often possible for a respondent to talk about his or her constructed realities in way that is totally satisfactory to the researcher, because the respondent, like the fish who would have a hard time describing water, is unlikely to be aware that the common language would evoke any constructions other than those that he or she is using.

For this reason the naturalistic researcher will gather data from a variety of sources and, preferably, in a variety of ways. Respondents are asked questions, but they are also encouraged to engage with the researcher in less structured conversations so that their hidden assumptions and constructions begin to surface. They are observed in their daily activity so that the researcher can begin to see the operational meaning of what they have said. Further insight into their constructed realities can be gained from documents that provide a historical context for interpreting their words and activity. Cluttered office arrangements, athletic award plaques on the wall, and spotless restrooms reflect values that helped shape the respondents' constructed realities. Data from all these sources are brought together and systematically analyzed in a process that proceeds parallel to data collection. Gradually, the expert naturalistic researcher is able to explicate the constructed realities of the respondents in a way that was impossible for them to do it. It is gratifying to the researcher, when, after reading the final report of a study, a respondent asks, "How did you know all that?"

Naturalistic research involves utilizing what one comes into the world with (i.e., the five senses plus intuition) to gather, analyze, and construct reality from data. The primary instrument in this type of research is the researcher him- or herself. Relying on all its senses, intuition, thoughts, and feelings, the human instrument can be a very potent and perceptive data-gathering tool. Moreover, the human brain is unparalleled and unrivaled in its countless complex functions and capabilities. Lincoln and Guba (1985) explain that naturalistic researchers prefer humans as the primary data-gathering instruments for the following reasons:

> [B]ecause it would be virtually impossible to devise a priori a nonhuman instrument with sufficient adaptability to encompass and adjust to the variety of realities that will be encountered; because of the understanding that all instruments interact with respondents and objects but that only the human instrument is capable of grasping and evaluating the meaning of that differential interaction; because the intrusion of instruments intervenes in the mutual shaping of other elements and that shaping can be appreciated and evaluated only by a human; and because all instruments are value-based and interact with local values but only the human is in a position to identify and take into account (to some extent) those resulting biases. (pp. 39-40)

Purposive Sampling

Central to naturalistic research is purposive sampling. Random or representative sampling is not preferred because the researcher's major concern is not to generalize the findings of the study to a broad population or universe but to maximize discovery of the heterogeneous patterns and problems that occur in the particular context under study. Purposive and directed sampling through human instrumentation increases the range of data exposed and maximizes the researcher's ability to identify emerging themes that take adequate account of contextual conditions and cultural norms.

Patton (1990) writes:

> The logic and power of purposeful sampling lies in selecting *information-rich* cases for study in depth. Information-rich cases are those from which one can learn a great deal about issues of central importance to the purpose of the research, thus the term *purposeful sampling*. For example, if the purpose of an evaluation is to increase the effectiveness of a program in reaching [lower] socioeconomic groups, one may learn a great deal more by focusing in-depth on understanding the needs, interests, and incentives of a small

number of carefully selected poor families than by gathering standardized information from a large, statistically representative sampling of the whole program. The purpose of purposeful sampling is to select information-rich cases whose study will illuminate the questions under study. (p. 169)

The researcher makes two basic decisions in purposive sampling. First, he or she must select who and what to study, that is, the sources that will most help to answer the basic research questions and fit the basic purpose of the study. Second, the researcher must choose who and what not to investigate; that is, there must be a process of elimination in order to narrow the pool of all possible sources.

Patton (1990) offers several different strategies for making decisions like the above. These include:

- *sampling extreme or deviant cases* obtains information about special or unusual cases that may be either troublesome or enlightening;
- *intensity sampling* examines cases that manifest the phenomenon intensely but not extremely (e.g., good students-poor students, above average-below average);
- *maximum variation sampling* consists of documenting unique variations that have emerged in adapting to different conditions;
- *homogeneous sampling* focuses, reduces variation, simplifies analysis, and facilitates group interviewing;
- *critical case sampling* permits maximum application and logical generalization of information to other cases;
- *criterion sampling* consists of picking all cases that meet some criterion, such as all children abused in a treatment facility;
- *opportunistic sampling* allows for following new leads during fieldwork, taking advantage of the unexpected, and flexibility;
- *random purposeful sampling* (still small sample size) adds credibility to a sample when the potential purposeful sample is larger than one can handle (not for generalizations or representativeness);
- *sampling politically important cases* attracts attention to the study (or avoids attracting undesired attention by purposefully eliminating from the sample politically sensitive cases); and
- *convenience sampling* saves time, money, and effort; poorest rationale and lowest credibility; yields information-poor cases.

Another aspect of purposive sampling is sample size. The basic rule is, "There are no rules for sample size." In qualitative research one is looking more for quality than quantity, more for information richness than information volume. For example, Patton (1990) reminds us that Piaget contributed to our understanding of how children think by observing his own two children at length and in-depth. Freud based his findings in psychoanalysis on fewer than 10 client cases. Peters and Waterman (1982) formulated their principles of organizational excellence on 62 companies.

Patton (1990) adds:

> In the end, sampling size adequacy, like all aspects of research, is subject to peer review, consensual validation, and judgment. What is crucial is that the sampling procedures and decisions be fully described, explained, and justified so that information users and peer reviewers have the appropriate context for judging the sample. The researcher or evaluator is absolutely obligated to discuss how the sample affected the findings, the strengths and weaknesses of the sampling procedures, and any other design decisions that are relevant for interpreting and understanding the reported results. (p. 186)

Patton believes that by using the directed power of a small purposive sample, and by not attempting to overgeneralize from it, the researcher can do much to allay fears about inadequate sample size.

An example of the thought process involved in purposive sampling can be seen in Maril's (1983) ethnographic study of Texas shrimpers:

> The in-depth interviews were continued in the summers of 1978, 1979, and 1980. A total of approximately 150 interviews from eight different ports was eventually collected. . . .
>
> Only shrimpers who regularly fish in the Gulf of Mexico were interviewed. Those fishermen who net shrimp in the Texas bays and channels were excluded from the sample. These bay shrimpers fish on a daily basis, returning to shore when the sun sets; their work on the water and their lives on land are very different from those of the men who fish for shrimp in the open gulf.
>
> Fifty-eight captains and captain-owners were interviewed, along with [48] riggers and [37] headers. From previous experience I knew that riggers and headers would be the most difficult to interview because they were the hardest to find; headers, in particular, are a marginal work force, often with limited social ties. Of equal importance, I recognized that riggers and headers, a significant number of whom were undocumented workers, were less likely to respond to an unknown interviewer. (pp. xv-xvi)

Data-Gathering Sources

In qualitative data gathering and analysis, attention should be given to constructing a comprehensive, holistic portrayal of the social and cultural dimensions of a particular context. In order to obtain this holistic qualitative portrayal, each case, site, or event is treated as a unique entity with its own particular meaning and its own constellation of relationships emerging from and related to the context in which it exists (Patton, 1990). It is the researcher's job to illuminate the obvious and subtle dimensions of this context. Bruyn (1966) challenges the participant observer "to seek the essence of the life of the observed, to sum up, to find a central unifying principle" (p. 316).

In the collection and analysis of data it is sometimes hard to distinguish between when the collecting ends and when the analysis begins, for gathering and analysis are complementary, ongoing, and often simultaneous processes. Nonetheless, the basic means and sources of data collection will be discussed in this chapter and data analysis will be developed in Chapter 6. There are basically four general sources that the researcher utilizes in naturalistic research: interviews, observations, documents, and artifacts.

Reflecting on his research done on the alcoholic experience, Denzin (1987) notes the contribution of these interactive sources:

> I weave life stories of self throughout my analysis, presenting alcoholics to the reader as they present themselves to fellow alcoholics. I also combine, in a variety of triangulated forms, a multiplicity of materials and methods including interviewing, observations, participation, archival analysis, textual criticism, semiotics, and the study of fictional and autobiographical accounts of alcoholism. (p. 24)

Interviews

Many think of interviews as one person (i.e., the researcher) asking questions and another (i.e., the subject) answering. However, in naturalistic research, interviews take more of the form of a dialogue or an interaction. Dexter (1970) describes interviews as a conversation with a purpose. Interviews allow the researcher and respondent to move back and forth in time; to reconstruct the past, interpret the present, and predict the future (Lincoln & Guba, 1985). Interviews also help the researcher to understand and put into a larger context the interpersonal, social, and cultural aspects of the environment. Fetterman (1989) writes:

> [Interviews] require verbal interaction, and language is the commodity of discourse. Words and expressions have different values in various cultures. People exchange these verbal commodities to communicate. The [re-searcher] quickly learns to savor the informant's every word for its cultural or subcultural connotations as well as for its denotative meaning. (p. 48)

Interviews may take a wide variety of forms, including a range from those that are very focused or predetermined to those that are very open-ended, and nothing is set ahead of time. Most common, however, is the semistructured interview that is guided by a set of basic questions and issues to be explored, but neither the exact wording nor the order of questions is predetermined (Merriam, 1988). Yin (1984) adds:

> Most commonly case study interviews are of an [open-ended] nature in which an investigator can ask key respondents for the facts of a matter as well as for the respondents' opinions about events. In some situations, the investigator may even ask the respondent to propose his or her own insights into certain occurrences and may use such propositions as the basis for further inquiry. (p. 83)

This open-ended or informal interviewing process is similar to and yet different from an informal conversation. The researcher and respondent dialogue in a manner that is a mixture of conversation and embedded questions. Fetterman (1989) further explains:

> The questions typically emerge from the conversation. In some cases they are serendipitous and result from comments by the participant. In most cases, the [researcher] has a series of questions to ask the participant and will wait for the most appropriate time to ask them during the conversation (if possible). (p. 49)

In his research in the federal penitentiary at Lompoc, California, when-ever Fleisher went into a cellblock, he never told prison personnel that they were being interviewed. "We 'just talked,' as I accompanied a hack or a counselor working as a hack on their regular duties" (Fleisher, 1989, p. 102).

However, one should not get the impression that interviews should be entered into lightly. Much thought and preparation should precede these purposeful conversations. There are several guidelines that can aid the researcher in the interviewing process.

One guideline is that the researcher and respondents should have a common vocabulary. Interviews require verbal interaction, and terminology and nuance need to be as clear and mutually understood as possible. Words and expressions have different significance in different cultures, and individuals exchange these verbal values to communicate. The researcher should identify those terms that are common to him or her and the culture under study as well as those terms that have multiple or divergent meanings. Furthermore, questions must be carefully worded in order to obtain pertinent information. Patton (1980) explains:

> Using words that make sense to the interviewee, words that reflect the respondents' world view, will improve the quality of data obtained during the interview. In many cases, without sensitivity to the impact of particular words on the person being interviewed, the answer may make no sense at all or there may be no answer. (p. 227)

The skilled interviewer can learn much from the words used by an interviewee that goes beyond the denotative meanings of those words. This skill is obviously a great asset to the naturalistic researcher who has acquired it. For the beginning researcher who wishes to develop this skill, we strongly recommend Spradley's *The Ethnographic Interview* (1979). As Spradley notes (p. 9), much of culture is encoded in linguistic form, and the researcher can learn much both from casual comments and lengthy interviews. This very practical, intensively focused book describes in detail how productive respondents can be identified, how productive relationships can be formed with respondents, and how inferences can be made from what a respondent says. It does an excellent job of showing how words make communication possible but often serve to hide key cultural meaning from the outsider. It describes how the outsider (researcher) can make inferences from the interviewee's words that open up previously hidden meanings.

The careful choice of words in a question is one of the most important decisions a researcher can make during an interview. Seymour (1988) gives two examples of qualitative studies in the field of marketing that illustrate this.

> In the recent Burger King/McDonald's comparative advertisements, Burger King claims that their flamebroiling was preferred over McDonald's frying by a margin of three to one. The key question was "Do you prefer your

hamburgers flame-broiled or fried?" Leo Shapiro, an independent researcher, decided to ask the question another way: "Do you prefer a hamburger that is grilled on a hot stainless-steel grill or cooked by passing the raw meat through an open gas flame?" The results to this question had 53 percent of the people preferring the McDonald's grilling process.

Elmo Roper, preparing to make a poll for *Fortune* magazine on attitudes toward governmental attempts to keep peace, pretested the following question: "Should the United States do all in its power to promote world peace?" Ninety-seven percent of the answers were in the affirmative. With a similar sample of respondents, the questions "Should the United States become involved in plans to promote world peace?" was responded to in the affirmative by only 60 percent of those questioned. (pp. 141-143)

In his study of prisons, Fleisher (1989, p. 12) found that the world inside the prison had its own vocabulary where the correctional officers called inmates "thugs" and themselves "hacks." The inmates often referred to themselves as "gangsters" (Fleisher, 1989, p. 114). In his study, a glossary was included with prison vocabulary used by inmates and staff members, such as *Crips* (a Los Angeles street gang), *fish* (a new inmate), *grill* (an iron-bar door), *ink* (a tattoo), *PC* (protective custody), and *post* (a work location).

The key to getting rich data from dialogue is in asking good questions and in careful listening and recording. It is important to prepare a list of carefully worded questions that reflect the basic research question and problem(s) of the study. However, the researcher must be careful not to be bound or overly structured by those questions and to allow them to naturally emerge over the course of the interview. Merriam (1988, pp. 78-79) cites Patton (1980) in delineating six basic kinds of questions that can be used to get different types of data:

1. Experience/behavior questions are aimed at eliciting descriptions of experiences, behaviors, actions, and activities (e.g., "What are some of the most memorable experiences you have had as an administrator?").

2. Opinion/value questions try to find out what people think. They tell us people's goals, intentions, desires, and values (e.g., "Why are you a teacher?").

3. Feeling questions are aimed at understanding emotional responses (e.g., "How did you feel when the administration moved you to a different grade level?").

4. Knowledge questions are aimed at factual information (e.g., "How many teachers are there in this school?").

5. Sensory questions determine what sensory stimuli—sight, sound, touch, taste, or smell—respondents are sensitive to (e.g., "Why do you like plants in your room?").

6. Background/demographic questions are aimed at understanding the respondent's education, previous experiences, age, residence, etc. (e.g., "Will you briefly explain your educational background?").

There are some types of questions that should be avoided. For instance, questions that cause an interviewee's response to be distorted or reactive should be avoided. An example of such a question might be "How do you feel about the principal firing you this year?" Merriam (1988) further advises:

> Avoid Multiple Questions—either one question that is actually a double question or a series of single questions that does not allow the respondent a chance to answer one by one (e.g., "How do you feel about the faculty and the courses in this school?"). . . . Leading questions should also be avoided. These set the respondent up to accept the researcher's point of view. The question "What emotional problems have you had since losing your job?" reflects a bias suggesting that anyone losing a job will have emotional problems. Finally, all researchers warn against asking yes/no questions. Any question that can be answered with a simple yes or no probably will be too simple to have value. (p. 80)

Ethical considerations should always be at the forefront of naturalistic research. The first element common to every protocol is the researcher's respect for the person and group under study. Ethical issues surrounding interviews include the researcher's motives and intentions as well as the study's purpose, the protection of respondents through the use of pseudonyms, establishing beforehand who has the final say over the study's content, and sensitivity to time and the number of interviewees involved in the study. There are sometimes unintended circumstances that could possibly bring harm to the respondent. There are occasions when the respondent is put in a vulnerable situation because of very sensitive data that emerge in the interview. Also, it is not uncommon for the researcher and respondent to form a type of relationship that gives the researcher privy information that could cause damage to the individual or group. Almost all strategies for data gathering have ethical dimensions. It would be well for the researcher to remember that in a naturalistic study the respondent should be considered a full partner in the study. The researcher's goal is to get behind the data being collected and to see through them the constructed realities of the respondent. After having been allowed into this very private world of the respondents, what possible right can the researcher claim to harm or destroy it?

Some of the best tools in recording interview data are the pen and legal pad. A list of predevised, carefully worded questions should be handy to review when necessary. The best way to enter into the interviews is basically the same way one would enter into a conversation: "How did you get into teaching?" "Tell me about yourself." "What do you really like about this school?" Take notes throughout the conversation, if possible, and allow some time after the interview to go to a quiet place to record your reactions and note any details you may have left out.

Fleisher (1989), in his study of prisons, never hid his pocket notebook and used it freely whenever he talked with someone, though at times, as when he was involved in a correctional task that required his attention or his physical involvement (for example, in shaking down an inmate), it was impossible for him to use it. Although the staff members of the prison did not object to his recording information in their presence, the same activity at first made the convicts nervous. Later, as they became comfortable with Fleisher's dual role, this was no longer a significant problem.

A well-organized plan, built around the central questions and issues that the interviewer wishes to explore, is a most important tool in a semistructured interview. The interviewer should have these written on paper, but they should also be indelibly printed in his or her mind. In this way the interviewer can take advantage of the situation when the respondent spontaneously drifts off into addressing a scheduled but as yet unasked question. It is extremely important to be able to take advantage of the respondent's spontaneity rather than stifling it in an attempt to keep the interview on track. Appropriate follow-up questions are asked to obtain additional needed information in the new area. Sometimes the interviewer may find it profitable to completely explore this parenthetical area before returning to the original issue. A well-articulated interview plan can afford the researcher this flexibility.

Many researchers advise the use of audio or video tape recorders. This ensures that everything said is captured on tape. Furthermore, the researcher can reflect on ways to improve his or her interviewing strategies after listening to or viewing a tape. One disadvantage of taped interviews is that the respondent is sometimes self-conscious or overly aware of the recorder. (However, this same fear, as Fleisher found when he took notes in the presence of inmates, could be directed toward the legal pad and pen. Personal discretion should be used here.) Another problem could be malfunctioning equipment. Many times researchers record interviews and simultaneously take notes in order to ensure quality and reliable data. Keep in mind that the flow of valid data must always take precedence. If the respondent is uncomfortable with equipment of any kind, then those inhibiting things must be put away so the flow of data will be unobstructed and continuous.

Conducting an interview involves several steps that are both sequential and interconnected. These necessary stages are the following: determining the respondents, preparing for the interview, beginning the interview, maintaining productivity during the interview, and bringing closure to the interview.

Determining the Respondents

Respondents are key figures in an interview. They are powerful figures because their perspective contributes greatly to the development of insight and understanding of the phenomenon. Sociologists speak of a good respondent as an informant, one who understands the culture but is also able to reflect on it and explain to the researcher what is going on (Merriam, 1988). The attitudes, orientation, and position of the interviewee are extremely important in shaping the total picture of the context. Therefore, the job of selecting a good informant is an important job of the researcher. A good informant is "one who can express thoughts, feelings, opinions, his or her perspective, on the topic being studied" (Merriam, 1988, p. 76).

Respondents are determined on the basis of what the researcher desires to know and from whose perspective that information is desired. Selecting individuals on the basis of what they can contribute to the understanding of the phenomenon under study means engaging in purposive sampling (Merriam, 1988). In the qualitative study of a school's strategies for teaching values, for example, a holistic picture of the educational program would involve the perceptions of a wide array of people, including teachers, students, parents, and community members.

The first respondent may be chosen because he or she has been nominated by a gatekeeper, because of his or her place of apparent prominence in the formal or informal structure, or even because of convenience to the researcher. As data collection from this individual reaches completion, a second respondent is chosen (often with the overt help of the first respondent) on the basis of what was learned from the first respondent. The process is repeated in choosing each new respondent. At first, respondents are chosen for the likelihood of their supplying new constructions to the researcher's understanding. Later in the process, respondents are more likely to be chosen for their perceived ability to elaborate or explicate constructions that have already been introduced. Thus, as Guba and Lincoln (1989) note, respondents are selected "serially" (one at a time) and "contingently" (based on what has been learned from previous respondents).

Preparing for the Interview

This step involves preparation for both the researcher and the respondent. The researcher must do his or her homework for the interview. This kind of preparation includes deciding on appropriate questions and their sequence, practicing the interview with an appropriate role stand-in, and deciding on the interviewer's own role, dress, level of formality, and the like (Lincoln & Guba, 1985). The researcher must also prepare the respondent in order for him or her to feel as comfortable and at ease as possible during the interview. Giving the interviewee pertinent information about the study, ensuring anonymity, explaining what will and will not be done with the data obtained in the interview, and confirming with the respondent the time and place of the interview can help the interviewee feel comfortable for the interview.

Beginning the Interview

Taylor and Bogdan (1984, pp. 87-88) suggest five issues that should be addressed at the beginning of every interview:

1. the investigator's motives and intentions and the inquiry's purpose
2. the protection of respondents through the use of pseudonyms
3. who has final say over the study's content
4. payment (if any)
5. the logistics of time and place and the number of interviews to be scheduled

Pleasantries and icebreakers are important in interviews and the respondent should be given time to warm up. Broad questions (e.g., "How did you get into education?" "Could you tell me a little about yourself?" "What are some things you like about your job?") give the interviewee a chance to relax and talk about nonthreatening topics.

Lincoln and Guba (1985) suggest that these "grand tour" questions "give the respondent practice in talking to the interviewer in a relaxed atmosphere while at the same time providing valuable information about how the respondent construes the general characteristics of the context" (p. 270).

Maintaining Productivity During the Interview

There are strategies that can enhance the quality of an interview. However, the best strategy is to be natural, to be oneself, during the interview. Fetterman (1989) concurs:

> Being natural is much more convincing than any performance. Acting like an adolescent does not win the confidence of adolescents, it only makes them suspicious. . . . First, ethnographic training emphasizes honesty in fieldwork including interviews. Deceptive games have no place in the interview setting or elsewhere. Second, . . . the objective is to learn from the interviewee, not to impress the person with how much the questioner already knows about the area. Third, even a consummate actor is bound to slip during a lengthy interview, and thus undermine all credibility. Being natural is the best protection. (p. 56)

A common procedure in interviewing is to start the interview with broad questions and become more specific as the interview progresses. There will be times when the interviewer will need to probe or pursue a certain line of thought with the respondent. Lincoln and Guba (1985) explain:

> The skilled interviewer is adept in the use of probes—directed cues for more or extended information. Probes may take the form of silence (respondents abhor an auditory vacuum, but it must be clear that the "talk turn" is with the respondent); "pumps"—sounds such as "uh-huh" or "umm" or encouraging waves of the hand; simple calls for more ("Could you tell me more about that?"); calls for examples; calls for reactions to the interviewer's reformulations of what was said ("Do I understand you to say that . . . "; or "If I understand you correctly, you seem to be saying that . . . "), or simply questions specifically formulated by the interviewer to embellish or extend something the respondent has said. (p. 271)

As Fetterman noted above, the interviewer should keep in mind that the person being interviewed is the expert on what he or she knows, understands, and feels. The interviewer's job is to access this rich store of data from the interviewee, not to impose, even inadvertently, his or her own interpretations or constructions. The interviewer should focus on obtaining the fullest picture that can be communicated of the interviewee's relevant constructions of reality.

Bringing Closure to the Interview

A positive beginning and conclusion to the interviewing process is essential. When concluding the interview, the interviewer should review or summarize what he or she understands to be the important parts of the interview; give the respondent ample opportunity to clarify or refine aspects that might cause confusion or dissatisfaction; thank the interviewee for his or her cooperation; and follow up the interview with a thank-you note that indicates the value of the respondent's information. Before terminating the interview, the researcher will often seek one additional piece of information from the respondent: the identification of other persons who might be valuable sources of information. By asking questions such as "Who else might have something to tell me about this topic?" or "Who would have a different view of this?" the researcher is often able to make use of an insider's knowledge to enrich his or her purposive sample. An extremely important principle of closure is to never bring final closure. That is, the interviewer should strive to always keep the doors of communication open between researcher and respondent. "If anything else comes to mind that you think would be important to the study, give me a call"; "I might be contacting you for further clarification a little later." Such simple expressions help to keep ongoing lines of communication open.

Interviews are valuable in data gathering. They allow the researcher to move back and forth in time as he or she probes and asks questions appropriate to the respondents' knowledge. They are useful in discovering what people think, how one person's perceptions compare with another's, and in putting those varying responses in the context of common group beliefs and themes (Fetterman, 1989).

Observations

The second source of data collection for the naturalistic researcher is observation. Marshall and Rossman (1989) define *observation* as "the systematic description of events, behaviors, and artifacts in the social setting chosen for study" (p. 79). Whereas interviews allow the researcher to travel, as it were, back and forth in time, observation allows the researcher to discover the here-and-now interworkings of the environment via the use of the five human senses. Guba and Lincoln (1981) explain the power in observation:

The basic methodological arguments for observation, then, may be summarized as these: [O]bservation . . . maximizes the inquirer's ability to
grasp motives, beliefs, concerns, interests, unconscious behaviors, cus-
toms, and the like; observation . . . allows the inquirer to see the world as
his subjects see it, to live in their time frames, to capture the phenomenon
in and on its own terms, and to grasp the culture in its own natural, ongoing
environment; observation . . . provides the inquirer with access to the emotional reactions of the group introspectively—that is, in a real sense it
permits the observer to use himself as a data source; and observation . . . allows the observer to build on tacit knowledge, both his own and that of
members of the group. (p. 193)

Observations, like interviews, can range from very focused to unstructured forms. In the early stages of the inquiry process the observations
should be less structured in order to permit the observer to expand his or
her tacit knowledge and to develop some sense of what is seminal or
salient (Lincoln & Guba, 1985). These types of observations can be compared
to taking a picture of the setting with a wide-angle camera lens. Where to
limit the scope of the picture should not be determined ahead of time, but
rather the focus must be allowed to develop and evolve over the course
of the study. One of the authors explains this process in a naturalistic
study, *Identifying Integrated Values Education Approaches in Secondary
Schools*:

I was amazed at the amount of significant, in-depth data I obtained merely
through careful observation. Nothing was too trivial or unimportant to
make note of. For example, the details of classroom decor, mannerisms of
teachers and students, empty classrooms (i.e., arrangement of chairs,
posters, books on shelves, etc.), nonverbal exchanges of students during
classroom lessons, interchange of students and teachers during lunch or
between class periods, the appearance of the hallways before and after
school, and many, many other fine points were assiduously noted. At nights
I would read my daily records and often be reminded of events, conversations, comments, and situations that I would add to the data. In effect, I was
taking a written photograph of the school with the sensitive, wide-angle
lens of my own eye. This process enabled me to capture the life of the
school as it was seen at the time, while causing minimal disturbance to the
natural setting. The focused conversations and interviews that followed in
the data-gathering process served to reinforce and clarify the total picture.
(Harris, 1991, p. 182)

This process of identifying the seminal and salient features, of "capturing the life" of the organization being observed, requires that fertile, productive observations in a naturalistic study be conducted over a sufficient period of time. In her study of diabetics, Mobley (1992) noted that time is also required to allow the observer to be integrated into the context being observed so that her presence itself is not a major stimulus of the observed behavior.

Observations may be classified in several ways, depending on the desired relationship between researcher and setting. Patton (1980) has developed a continuum for thinking about one's role and relationship during the conduct of qualitative research. At one end of the continuum is the complete participant, who is a full member of the group and yet conceals his or her observer role from the group. At the other extreme is the complete observer, who either covertly observes the group from afar or is camouflaged in a completely public setting such as a restaurant or airport. There is a large degree of secrecy in both of these extremes, and a raft of ethical issues surround covert research. Lincoln and Guba (1985) comment that "ethics demand that covertness be eschewed except in very exceptional circumstances" (p. 274).

In most instances the naturalistic researcher will choose a role somewhere in the middle of this continuum as either participant-observer or observer-participant. In the participant-observer role the researcher's activities, which are known to the group, are subordinate to the researcher's role as a participant. A classic example of participant observation can be seen in Maril's (1983) study.

To understand the shrimpers' jobs from their viewpoint, Maril (1983) spent three weeks during the summer of 1977 working as a shrimp header in the Gulf of Mexico. Although he found the work nearly impossible at first, he gradually learned to head shrimp at a reasonable rate. He also cooked meals, cleaned the boat, and sometimes stood watch at the wheel while other crew members were busy with their jobs. Although his fellow crew members never forgot that he was not completely one of them, the common demands of tasks at sea bonded the four of them together as friends and workers. From this vantage point Maril was able to comprehend and feel firsthand the shrimpers' anxieties about the economic uncertainties of shrimping and their feelings about the long periods away from home and family. During this period of participant observation, he kept a systematic log of everything that occurred aboard the trawler. This and the three-week intense experience provided him with insights and constructions of reality that he could never have gained from land-based shrimpers or even from interviewing these same crew members when they returned to land.

In the observer-participant mode the researcher's participation in the group is secondary to his or her role as an information gatherer (Merriam, 1988). In reality, one may vacillate between these intermediate roles or seek to find a balance. Merriam (1988) concisely presents the pertinent issues involved in such a decision:

> A question can be raised as to just how much better it is to be an insider. Being born into a group, "going native," or just being a member does not necessarily afford the perspective necessary for studying the phenomenon. Jarvie (1982, p. 68) notes that "there is nothing especially privileged about the observation of a parade made by those in it. Spectators are in a better position. . . . " On the other hand, Swisher (1986) was able to get reliable information about multicultural education from parents and teachers in a reservation community because she herself is a member of the community. Patton (1980, p. 128) underscores the balance needed . . . : "Experiencing the program as an insider is what necessitates the participant part of participant observation. At the same time, however, there is clearly an observer side of the process. The challenge is to combine participation and observation so as to become capable of understanding the program as an insider while describing the program for outsiders." (pp. 93-94)

It is impossible to observe and record everything in a setting, and therefore one must begin somewhere with some type of plan. Merriam (1988) has compiled the following checklist of elements likely to be present in an observation.

1. The setting: What is the physical environment like? What is the context? What kinds of behavior does the setting promote or prevent?

2. The participants: Describe who is in the scene, how many people, and their roles. What brings these people together? Who is allowed here?

3. Activities and interactions: What is going on? Is there a definable sequence of activities? How do the people interact with the activity and with one another? How are people and activities connected or interrelated?

4. Frequency and duration: When did the situation begin? How long does it last? Is it a recurring type of situation or is it unique? If it recurs, how frequently? How typical of such situations is the one being observed?

5. Subtle factors: Less obvious but perhaps as important to the observation are:

- informal and unplanned activities
- symbolic and connotative meanings of words
- nonverbal communication such as dress and physical space
- unobtrusive measures such as physical clues
- what does not happen—especially if it ought to have happened.

Much has been written on the importance and how-to's of interviews in qualitative research, and comparatively little attention has been given to the fine art of observation. Interviews are, no doubt, significant in naturalistic inquiry. However, most adults have lost much of the natural ability to learn by careful and intuitive observation. Much is to be gained by looking, listening, feeling, and smelling rather than by merely talking. Many fine and important details have become obscured in the day-to-day activities of life. The development and refinement of the underestimated art of observation should be a primary emphasis in the practice of naturalistic research.

The beginning researcher should devise a system for recording observations. There are many observation schedules for observing specific types of human interaction; most focus on fairly narrow aspects (e.g., oral interaction in a classroom). There are also various schedules for data that can be observed about architectural characteristics, personal reactions, and other aspects of a social context. The beginning researcher is encouraged to examine these tools and probably construct his or her own to fit a particular social context.

Video equipment is sometimes used in observations, but it is possible that a camera may be too obtrusive in some cases and bias the respondents' actions or comments. When filming equipment is used, an adjustment period, an initial length of time in which no data are gathered, may be necessary. Seymour (1988) notes:

> In a recent study for Kimberly-Clark, a researcher video taped some 200 hours of diaper changing techniques to assist in a redesign of "Huggies." The researcher noted that "People played to the camera first, but it soon became just another part of their daily lives." An illustration is [also] available in the study for the utility company in which cameras were placed in people's homes in order to observe the details of thermostat setting: [T]he researcher made no attempt to gather data until several weeks after the cameras had been installed. (p. 71)

Interaction Between Interviews and Observations

The naturalistic researcher should realize that interviews and observations build understanding of a social context in an interactive way. For this reason, the researcher cannot treat these two human sources of data as independent of each other. The interactive process that joins them parallels the relationship between experience, language, and constructed realities that we discussed in Chapter 2. Interviews and observations have a reciprocal relationship similar to that by which language and experience structure and enrich each other. As Helen Keller noted, " [T]he more I handled things and learned their names, the more joyous and confident grew my sense of kinship with the rest of the world" (1954, p. 37). Through interviews, the researcher often gains a first insight into the constructed realities that are wrapped up in the idiolect of the respondent. Through observations, the researcher gains a partially independent view of the experience on which the respondent's language has constructed those realities. The interview provides leads for the researcher's observations. Observation suggests probes for interviews. The interaction of the two sources of data not only enriches them both, but also provides a basis for analysis that would be impossible with only one source. Just as this interactive relationship reflects the more basic relationship among language, experience, and thought, it also looks forward to the entire process of naturalistic analysis that we will describe in Chapter 6 in the section on the hermeneutic-dialectic method.

Documents

Documents constitute a third source of evidence. The term *document* refers to the broad range of written and symbolic records, as well as any available materials and data. Documents include practically anything in existence prior to and during the investigation, including historical or journalistic accounts, works of art, photographs, memos, accreditation records, television transcripts, newspapers, brochures, meeting agendas and notes, audio- or videotapes, budget or accounting statements, notes from students or teachers, speeches, and other case studies.

The data obtained from documents can be used in the same manner as those derived from interviews or observations. Although one should not impose self-limitations on the quantity or quality of available documents during the initial stages of the investigative process, some discernment and intuition should come into play in document gathering or one will accrue mountains of analytical headaches. For example, one would not consider all the books and magazine articles in a library as possible sources for documents or literature review tools. There must be some tacit and rational screening process involved.

The search for documents is guided by the researcher's emerging design. Merriam (1988) notes that it is a flexible yet systematic process that allows the researcher's hunches and tentative hypotheses to serve as guides in the "accidental" discovery of valuable data. She observes that this process, using both skill and intuition, is not essentially different from that used in interviews or observations.

Artifacts

Another important source of evidence for naturalistic research is the material artifacts of a research setting that give insight into the culture's technology, social interaction, and physical environment. Artifacts can be technological devices (e.g., computer printouts and disks), works of art, writing instruments, tools, and almost any other physical evidence. Detailed studies of artifacts are necessary if a researcher is to explore the systematic relationship between people and their physical environment. Yin (1984) gives an example of one study of the actual versus the espoused use of microcomputers in the classroom:

> Although utilization could be directly observed, an artifact—the computer printout—was also available. Students displayed these printouts as the finished product of their work and maintained notebooks of the printouts. Each printout showed not only the type of schoolwork that had been done but also the date and amount of computer time used to do the work. By examining the printouts, the case study investigators were able to develop a broader perspective concerning all of the classroom applications, beyond that which could be directly observed in a short period of time. (p. 89)

Human and Nonhuman Sources of Data

We have described four types of data sources: interviews, observations, documents, and artifacts. The first two of these might be categorized as "human sources" and the latter two as "nonhuman sources," although this may be a little misleading because documents and artifacts of interest will generally have their origins in human thought or activity. Another way of categorizing these sources might be as "stable" (documents and artifacts) and "dynamic" (interviews and observations). This categorization suggests something about their interrelationship.

We have spent more time in this chapter exploring the human sources, chiefly because they are dynamic. They are changing and reactive to the presence and initiatives of the researcher. Because of this the researcher must take measures not simply to follow a plan for collecting the data that these sources hold, but also to plan for unseen contingencies that will affect the plan and open up new and unanticipated vistas of information. The researcher must develop strategies for discovering the codes that will unlock the data that these human sources hold. These sources are not only repositories of rich information, but also themselves autonomous and often unpredictable generators of information. Seldom, if ever, has the full potential of human sources been totally exhausted by a researcher.

There is also much rich information hidden in documents and artifacts that often goes untapped by researchers, but it does not react to the researcher's presence or initiatives. As a result, these stable nonhuman sources provide a context for understanding and evaluating the data obtained from dynamic human sources. Thus the two types of data sources, human and nonhuman, interact with each other as figure and ground in a manner that expands their overall meaning while obscuring the distinction between figure and ground (Hofstadter, 1980).

Denzin's (1987) description of his data-gathering methods illustrates the dynamic interaction of human and nonhuman sources:

> My materials are drawn from a five-year period of study, primarily in a medium-sized community of 150,000. . . . I have observed the workings of A.A. in over 2,000 open and closed meetings. I have gathered observations from substance abuse treatment centers and detoxification programs. I have had discussions and interviews with active and recovering alcoholics and their family members. . . . I have also had conversations with treatment personnel, physicians, psychiatrists, social workers, hospital emergency room nurses. . . . I have examined the literature of Alcoholics Anonymous . . . and numerous materials printed and distributed by the World Service of A.A. (p. 21)

Data collection methods in a naturalistic study often assume the qualities of the various strands of color and shape in a rich tapestry. The balance of one method with others derives from and at the same time gives shape to the emerging design. Chace (1992) illustrates this integration of data collection methods in recounting his study of interpretive restraint in the annual Bok Kai Festival in the city of Marysville, California:

> My wife and I attended the weekend Marysville's Bok Kai Festival to document the Chinese folk religious ritual forms within one contemporary California community. . . . We observed and made notes on these major events, photodocumented most of the activities, and conducted informal interviews with local organizers and participants. We devoted ourselves to an intensive weekend, recognizing that this ritual celebration occurs only once each year. Each of us moved around independently to make observations in various locations from different vantages. Intermittently, during festival activities and through the evenings, we compared and debated our observations and commentaries, which both reinforced our understanding of activities and highlighted differences in our experiences.
>
> To supplement our observations and casual interviews, we collected the various printed materials produced for the festival activities. The most important of these were the Bok Kai parade announcers' 28-page script, the local chamber of commerce announcements, and the plethora of festival promotion and reportage in the local newspapers. Additionally, we secured the 18-page pictorial booklet that the community had produced 20 years earlier to help support the Bok Kai Temple and which included brief historical notes. These sources were important, for we found that they contained the knowledge held by many community members, and in our interviews, people often simply repeated this information to us.
>
> After the festival, we conducted further interviews with Chinese Americans and Anglo-Americans who lived or had previously lived in Marysville or had attended past festivals there. These interviews addressed more specific issues in our understanding and interpretation of the ritual events. Additionally, we were able to arrange to return and further photodocument the temple. (pp. 10-11)

Recording Data

As we observed in our earlier discussion of interview techniques, the recording of data as it is gathered often presents a dilemma for the researcher. Ideally, the researcher would like to have records that provide the most accurate description possible of the critical events in the research setting. However, although accuracy can be improved by using a tape recorder or taking notes as the events occur, the obtrusiveness of these strategies often prevents the researcher from using them. In some settings, their use might effectively seal the researcher off from access to additional data. There is no fixed prescription for the researcher to follow, though the general advice to the researcher is simple: "Gather data in a manner that presents the most complete picture of what has happened in the research setting, but never allow your data collection procedures to cut you off from access to additional data that you may need."

In her treatise on battered women and shelters, Loseke (1992) explains her resolution of the dilemma:

> I have two primary forms of data for this analysis. The first are notes from the shelter logbook, a worker-written ongoing commentary about life inside South Coast. This organizational document was compiled by workers and only workers could read its contents. The log served the practical purpose of allowing communication among revolving shifts of workers, who rarely saw one another but who were engaged in the common task of shelter work. . . .
>
> My field notes are the second major form of data I will be using. These notes sometimes are from staff meetings where workers allowed me to tape their deliberations, some are from interactions with workers or clients I managed to transcribe verbatim since I take shorthand. Yet most of my several hundred pages of field notes are not so detailed. I decided quite early that many of the most critical happenings at South Coast could not be turned into data collection events. For example, although I witnessed several client selection decisions and, in fact, was responsible for a few myself, I neither took notes nor turned on my tape recorder during these times. Nor did I take notes while listening to workers and clients talk. I always went home or to my office and reconstructed what I had seen or experienced. (pp. 168-169)

One general technique that we have found especially helpful for recording human behavior in social contexts is the construction of critical incidents. As we use the term, a *critical incident* has two defining characteristics:

1. It is a specific event occurring in the social context being studied.
2. It should reflect "critically" on the operation of that context.

"Critical" here means that the incident reflects on a significant feature of the social context being studied. Critical events are those that either highlight the normal operation of the school organization or contrast sharply with it. This immediately raises the question, "How does the researcher recognize a critical incident?" At first, in a new social context, the researcher has no better direction than his or her previous familiarity with social settings. At first glance, this may seem totally inadequate because of the uniqueness of each social setting. However, there are enough similarities in human behavior and interpersonal patterns across contexts to give nearly any researcher enough background to begin collecting critical incidents.

In fact, one of the most useful features of critical-incident collection is that, in the early days in a setting, an observer cannot really tell whether an observed event should be considered a normal event (i.e., one that exemplifies what is central to the social context) or one in sharp contrast to it (i.e., one that identifies the boundaries of the context). Conjectures about whether an event is central or bounding lead to the formation of testable working hypotheses that give direction to the study. For instance, imagine that you are studying a junior high school and that on the first day of your study you are standing with the principal in an otherwise empty hallway when suddenly a 12-year-old boy comes around the corner and runs past you. What the principal does at this point will tell something about the school. If she calls after the young man, makes a note for future reference, or totally ignores the situation, you as the observer have learned something about the school. Even a novice researcher should recognize that this event reflects on the operation of the school. The chief question now is whether what you've observed is the rule or the exception. The collection of many more critical incidents will answer this question in a way that may lead to rich insights about the constructed realities that operate in the school.

The critical incident should be recorded in *descriptive* terms that are as specific as possible. The two greatest weaknesses of many critical-incident descriptions are (1) that they are written in judgmental terms and (2) that they attempt to summarize too much and are too general. Consider these critical-incident descriptions:

1. The principal has periodically discussed potential truancy problems with his two assistants who have recommended that he take a firm stand to prevent them.

2. Mr. A., the principal, and his two assistants are discussing what to do with a new student who is a potential truancy problem. Mr. B., the assistant principal for administration, whose style is very authoritarian and who is very rigid in his attitudes toward students, states somewhat angrily that he has threatened both the student and his parents that he will not hesitate to turn the matter over to the courts if there's any trouble.

3. Mr. A., the principal, Mr. B., the assistant principal for administration, and Ms. C., the assistant principal for guidance, are in a conference one afternoon in Mr. A's office. The discussion turns to a new student who has been accepted into the school despite a truancy record at previous schools. Mr. B. says, rather loudly, "I've made it clear to the student and his parents that we expect attendance. We'll accept the student as long as attendance is maintained. If it isn't, we'll make it a court case."

Description 1 summarizes too much and is too general. Description 2 is too judgmental. Description 3 is closest to what a critical-incident description should be like. In addition, a critical incident should have the following characteristics:

1. It should contain only one event or chief description.
2. It should identify persons, locations, and times as specifically as possible.
3. It should either be observed by the writer or be verifiable by more than one source.
4. It should help define the operation of the organization by focusing on either a typical event or one that is distinctively atypical.

With these principles in mind, the researcher who wishes to use the critical-incident technique should just get started. We recommend that the critical incidents be recorded on index cards, each on a separate card. Date and time of day should be referenced on one corner of the card. Many of the new researcher's early recorded critical incidents will not follow all the recommendations that we have made. This is not too important. By regularly reviewing his or her incidents for format and usability, the researcher will be able to adapt the system for his or her own research purposes. One clear benefit for the researcher will be a mode of recording that is suitable for a broad range of significant data and will greatly facilitate the analysis process.

The use of critical incidents to understand social contexts and to uncover the constructions developed by those who operate in them has been described by one of the authors of this text (Erlandson, 1979, 1992). He found that by collecting sets of critical incidents on schools and other human service organizations (or by asking the individuals in those organizations to collect critical incidents) he was able to use those sets to effectively communicate the essence of those organizations to persons on the outside. Specifically, he asked individuals not familiar with an organization to use a set of critical incidents to make inferences about what was happening in the organization and about beliefs held by members of the organization, even when this information was not specifically mentioned in the critical incidents. He also asked them to make predictions about what would happen in the organization in the future. Inferences were then checked with members of the organization; in some cases, the passage of time made it possible to check on predictions that were made. The inferences made by persons whose only knowledge of the organization was what they had read in the collection of separate incidents was remarkably close to the information given by organization members. In those cases where it was possible to check on predictions about the organization, striking similarities were also found. What seemed to be happening was that the separate incidents, while each revealing a relatively discrete piece of information, together produced a web that captured and communicated many organizational regularities and interdependencies. Particularly interesting was the ability of persons who were previously unaware of the organization to tell members of the organization things that were not mentioned on the critical incident cards and which members of the organization had assumed were inside secrets.

We have found the critical-incident technique to be a very useful and comprehensive tool for recording data. While particularly suitable for recording observed events, the tool can also record events described in interview notes. In fact, it may also record what happened during the interview itself, such as providing a description of how an interviewee related two events that the researcher had previously thought were unrelated or of the reaction of an interviewee to a piece of information. Documented events, such as a meeting or a bureaucratic decision, may also be included by providing a brief outline or summary of a letter or the minutes of a meeting on an index card, which is then referenced back to the original document. The collection of critical incidents parallels the procedure we have described for determining respondents for interviews. Just as those respondents were chosen first for their ability to provide diverse information and then for their ability to elaborate and explicate emerging themes, critical incidents focus attention on events that identify the boundaries of the social context and those that elaborate its center. Our experience has indicated that the human computer is a wonderful instrument for sensing, after only a limited time in the social context, that an event is either bounding or central to the context.

We have found the critical-incidents technique to be an effective central tool for recording and organizing the events of a naturalistic study. Accompanied by a log that records what is happening to the researcher him- or herself, the critical-incidents technique (supported, of course, by the documents and interview notes that they reference) has been the only recording strategy we have used in some of our studies. By being recorded as single events, critical incidents facilitate ongoing analysis (as we shall see in Chapter 6). They also provide an excellent foundation for an audit trail (described in Chapter 7).

The Relationship of Thinking and Feeling

The human instrument is a wonderful data-processing organism. It is more sensitive to various shades of meaning and more able to appropriately respond to them than the most elaborate nonhuman instruments that might be imagined. However, its sensitivity and flexibility derive from its ability to interact with the data it encounters, and this interaction means that it will be affected, sometimes positively and sometimes adversely, by these encounters. These interaction effects tend to be particularly powerful during the first days of the study while the researcher is learning the context, but they will recur at various times throughout the study. The seasoned researcher will recognize these high and low emotional periods for what they are—the necessary adjustments of the wonderfully sensitive human instrument.

Johnson (1975) describes the relationship of thinking to feeling. As a researcher enters the research field, his or her private fears, apprehensions, feelings of ignorance, confusion, and incompetence impact the thought processes including the ability to collect and analyze data accurately. Johnson believes that it is perhaps useful to delay making any recordings until several weeks of the project has passed and anxieties have subsided. Johnson reports that in his research he made notes during this time of confusion and later found them not to be especially valuable in terms of either description or insight. He found the notes to be trivial and naive because of his ignorance of the setting and its tasks and the official rules of the context. Fieldworkers generally agree that the initial anxious feelings eventually subside, but this does not necessarily mean all goes smoothly thereafter. The following excerpt is from Johnson's notes recorded during the 10th week of his research:

> Also had a talk with Buzz this afternoon. I began by asking him what had happened recently with the kids at the Young Foster home, where we were last week. Buzz began his account by saying "Oh wow, J.J., you wouldn't

believe how bad I blew it," and then he proceeded to describe the details of what he called his own ignorance, unprofessional conduct, erroneous judgments . . . and so on. Now I'll admit that I don't know all there is to know about social workers or social casework, but I . . . know enough about it to know . . . that there isn't a social worker . . . who would see that as unprofessional conduct. . . . He's one of the brightest guys I've met so far. . . . It's fairly obvious he was giving me some short-con this afternoon. . . . The thing today really got to me. After taking leave of the situation, I walked out of the office and over to the parking lot whereupon I proceeded to break into a cold sweat, felt weak-kneed and nauseous. (pp. 153-154)

This excerpt illustrates one researcher's private feelings and physical manifestations. He went to the parking lot to pull himself together and reconstruct a rational appearance. Sometimes it may be necessary to delay for a day or two writing the notes from a particularly emotional event in order to write a straightforward, properly balanced account. This example also shows that there exists the possibility of a gap between one's rational presentation and one's private feelings. In addition to exiting from the context temporarily, peer debriefing, which is discussed in Chapter 7, can help the researcher deal more effectively with the inevitable tension between thinking and feeling.

A record needs to be kept on the primary human instrument that is being used in the naturalistic study. This instrument is sensitive and actively responds to the setting being studied. This human instrument, the researcher, is governed by both thoughts and emotions and will certainly change, and hopefully grow, throughout the study. Some record of this change is needed, both because it is important to note the interaction with the setting and because the researcher's growth, along with that of the setting's stakeholders, is an important product of the research. For this purpose, we recommend a simple daily log to which each researcher can add his or her own special features, one that documents the researcher's own feelings, attitudes, learnings, and insights and which chronicles the researcher's growth over time.

Summary

Glaser and Strauss (1967) suggest two important requirements in the development of theory in inductive analysis: "(1) parsimony of variables and formulation, and (2) scope in the applicability of the theory to a wide range of situations" (pp. 110-111). The simultaneous analysis and data collection that occur in naturalistic studies allow the researcher to direct the data collection phase more productively, as well as develop a data base that is both parsimonious and relevant.

Interviews, observation, and the collection of documents and artifacts bring together multiple perspectives and allow the researcher to better understand the whole, the essence, through the use of his or her senses. One metaphor that describes this is known as *grokking*. McCarthy (1991) explains:

> The term . . . derives from the popular science fiction novel *Stranger in a Strange Land*, written in the 1960s by Robert Heinlein. The hero of the book, a human being born and raised on Mars, returns to Earth with some remarkable powers, including the ability to "grok." As the hero explains, "Grok means to drink . . . to understand thoroughly. . . . " The term is a metaphor for a profound concept and experience: the ability to understand something completely, to get it in an intuitive, "aha!" way. (p. 219)

Human beings are born with the ability to "grok," to drink in a vast amount of information and make sense and order of that information. The processes involved in gathering data in naturalistic research allow the researcher to rediscover the joys and adventures of intuitive learning.

For Further Study

1. Review two or more studies you have read that generally follow the naturalistic paradigm. Describe the various data collection methods that were used. Explain how these methods complemented and supported one another.

2. Choose a human interaction setting for observation (this may be a classroom, an office, a restaurant, a library, or some similar setting that is reasonably confined). Select a period of the day to observe this setting when there is likely to be a reasonable degree of human interaction. Then observe this setting for a period of 30 minutes, making notes on what is seen, heard, smelled, and felt. Finally, incorporate these observations in a series of "critical incidents" placed on 3×5 cards.

3. Use the critical incidents formulated in Question 2 as the basis for designing an open-ended interview with persons in the setting. Conduct at least two interviews with persons in the setting. Use the information gained from these interviews, that recorded on your critical incidents, and any additional information from documents and records to write a 3-to-5-page

summary of your observations and insights. Retain your critical incidents, interview data, documents and records, and summary paper for future use.

4. For the naturalistic study you are designing, determine what data you will collect and what methods you will use to collect them. Describe how these data collection methods are related to one another and to the overall purpose of the study.

6

≡

Data Analysis

THE ANALYSIS OF qualitative data is best described as a progression, not a stage; an ongoing process, not a one-time event. Marshall and Rossman (1989) explain:

> Data analysis is the process of bringing order, structure, and meaning to the mass of collected data. It is a messy, ambiguous, time-consuming, creative, and fascinating process. It does not proceed in a linear fashion; it is not neat. Qualitative data analysis is a search for general statements about relationship among categories of data; it builds grounded theory. (p. 112)

The analysis of the data gathered in a naturalistic inquiry begins the first day the researcher arrives at the setting. The collection and analysis of the data obtained go hand-in-hand as theories and themes emerge during the study. This process can be clearly seen in the following excerpt from the analysis section of a naturalistic study (Harris, 1991):

> The site visits [at the two schools] began in the early part of the 1990 spring semester. The initial visits consisted of broad exploration of the individual schools. Interviews and observations were recorded on a legal pad and later transferred along with data from documents to 3×5 note cards with separate units of information placed on separate cards. . . . Data analysis occurred throughout this research project. The sources of the data were interviews, documents, nonverbal cues, and other qualitative or quantitative information

pools. Inductive analysis was used to sort the data into categories that provided descriptive or inferential information about the context or setting from which the units were derived. Individual 3×5 cards with specific units of information were sorted and placed into provisional categories on the basis of "look-alike" characteristics. As these provisional categories began to accumulate substantial numbers of unit cards, the inquirer wrote a statement or category label that served as the basis of inclusion/exclusion decisions. (pp. 54-58)

The constant comparative method described by Glaser and Strauss (1967) was utilized in this study as a means for deriving (grounding) theory in the analysis process. From the categories, grounded theories—that is, theories that follow from data rather than preceding them—were developed. Glaser and Strauss (1967) further explain this method:

> This constant comparison of the incidents very soon starts to generate theoretical properties of the category. The analyst starts thinking in terms of the full range of types or continua of the category, its dimensions, the conditions under which it is pronounced or minimized, its major consequences, its relation to other categories, and its other properties. (p. 106)

Durst, Wedemeyer, and Zurcher (1985) used the constant comparative method in their study of parental partnerships in postdivorce families. The small number (21) of couples in their study enabled them to focus on adaptive strategies that work for divorced families and to use the constant comparative method to derive a theoretical perspective grounded in the research data. Their research methodology proceeded by rating and comparing incidents and responses that recurred in open-ended data in order to integrate them with other incidents. A conceptual frame took shape as patterns and themes were identified. The themes that emerged, although not conclusive, provided a plausible framework for future research on the postdivorce family.

In his study of worker behavior, Hodson (1991) also chose the constant comparative method to analyze the data he obtained from his unstructured interviews and observations and to break out of the theoretical straitjackets typically imposed on such studies. He explains his use of the method:

> In developing this data base, I relied on the principle of constant comparison in which the most recent responses are compared with previous responses in the search for consistencies, discrepancies, anomalies, and negative cases (Glaser, 1965; McCall & Simmons, 1969). After each interview, I transcribed

the interview verbatim and filed its material according to the categorization then in use. The material was typically in the form of paragraphs [that] were cross-classified to several categories. As I filed each statement, I compared it with previous statements in that category and kept running notes on the content of the category. The categories changed over time; some disappeared and were merged under more general titles. Some emerged out of previous categories that became too heterogeneous. Some categories became parts of matched pairs or triads in which any given comment would typically be filed in each constituent category. For example, comments [that] described instances of lax work or bad workmanship also typically mentioned abusive management. Similarly, statements that described devising one's own procedures also typically included statements of satisfaction with the autonomy that provided. This helped to reveal connections between categories.

I called this process to a halt when I felt that additional interviews were yielding little new information. (pp. 50-51)

Miles and Huberman (1984, p. 21) state, "We consider that analysis consists of three concurrent flows of activity: data reduction, data display, and conclusion drawing/verification." This interactive process in data analysis is a theme that is stated time and again in the writings of Glaser and Strauss (1967) cited above, as well as in those of Lincoln and Guba (1985) and the current authors. Although we take exception to the methods of data reduction and data display presented by Miles and Huberman (1984), we join the chorus of voices in proclaiming that data analysis does not occur in a vacuum. It must be in the forefront of the researcher's mind that data analysis occurs during data collection as well as after data analysis. The concept of looking at phenomena, stepping back and analyzing them, and drawing conclusions based on the resulting analysis is one of the major trappings of traditional research. Data analysis in a naturalistic project must include the interactive process of collection and analysis as well as the forming of a gestalt at the conclusion of the project.

The Interactive Process of Data Analysis

Data analysis in a naturalistic inquiry involves a twofold approach. The first aspect involves data analysis at the research site during data collection. The second aspect involves data analysis away from the site following a period of data collection. Note that this second aspect is conducted between site visits prior to as well as after completion of data collection.

As noted in Chapter 5, data analysis is closely tied with data collection. As mentioned above, a traditional study separates data collection from data analysis; a naturalistic study involves an inseparable relationship between data collection and data analysis. An assumption of the naturalistic researcher is that the human instrument is capable of ongoing fine tuning in order to generate the most fertile array of data. One effect of this continuous adjustment process is that as data are gathered, they are analyzed. Data analysis frequently necessitates revisions in data collection procedures and strategies. These revisions yield new data that are then subjected to new analysis. The result of this process is the effective collection of rich data that generate alternative hypotheses and provide the basis for shared constructions of reality.

This principle of interaction between data collection and analysis is one of the major features that distinguishes naturalistic research from traditional research; it probably cannot be overemphasized. The human instrument responds to the first available data and immediately forms very tentative working hypotheses that cause adjustments in interview questions, observational strategies, and other data collection procedures. New data, obtained through refined procedures, test and reshape the tentative hypotheses that have been formed and further modify the data collection procedures. This interactive refining process never really ceases until the final report has been written. Even in the final member check (see Chapter 7), interpretations are challenged and modified if the weight of data supports modification.

Although much of this interactive process is governed by the intuition of the researcher and, to the outside observer, seems to occur naturally when practiced by a seasoned naturalistic researcher, it should never be left to chance. The fledgling naturalistic researcher should consciously initiate the process at the end of every interview, at the end of every observation period, and certainly at the end of every day in the field setting. Key questions must be asked: What did I learn from this respondent that will shape my questions for the next respondent? What hypotheses have emerged that suggest additional questions, additional respondents, or a follow-up interview with this respondent? What are the major working hypotheses that are emerging from my observations? What data have I picked up that challenge these hypotheses? How can I modify my observational techniques to amplify, extend, or shift my working hypotheses? How can I be more efficient and effective in collecting and analyzing data?

The research of one of the authors required a 300-mile, round-trip commute between the schools being studied and his home. He would typically spend two consecutive days per week at whichever school he was studying and the remainder of the week back home at the university analyzing the data he had collected. On each return trip home, the researcher would set his voice-activated tape recorder on "record" and verbalize his thoughts, working hypotheses, unanswered questions, uncertainties, and ideas for further refinement of his data collection strategies. This had the effect of being a "talking" reflexive journal. The researcher was then able to review the tapes later, make notes about needed data, and be better prepared for his next site visit.

In conducting data analysis during data collection, the researcher utilizes some of the same methodological tools that ensure the study's trustworthiness (see Chapter 7); these are listed below.

1. *Triangulation.* By this method, the researcher seeks out several different types of sources that can provide insights about the same events or relationships. For example, if a teacher reports that school attendance has dropped significantly over the past two years, the researcher may review attendance documents in an effort to explicate the factual base that stimulated the report. If teachers report that student apathy is accelerating, the researcher may interview activities directors, students, and other school personnel to get their input on student apathy. The researcher may also analyze rosters of club membership, content of student publications, and other sources separate from the teachers' reports of apathy. Triangulation may establish that the information gathered is generally supported or disconfirmed; more important, however, it enhances meaning through multiple sources and provides for thick description of relevant information that, in the case of the example cited, may suggest reasons for the increased apathy.

2. *Development of working hypotheses.* Through this approach, the researcher reviews data collected and forms hypotheses about the phenomena studied. In essence, this amounts to "looking at your fish" to determine what themes emerge or recur. The data are sorted through in a variety of ways resulting in a variety of interpretations. The researcher selects the hypotheses that seem to best represent the constructions presented by the data sources. In a study on workers in the workplace, Hodson (1991) started his research thinking that he was studying organizational sabotage. After his preliminary observations and interviews, his hypothesis focused on subtle noncompliance, foot dragging, and conditional effort.

3. *Testing of working hypotheses.* The researcher tests the working hypotheses developed in order to determine their viability. For example, if

a body of data collected in a variety of ways leads the researcher to the hypothesis that the principal's style of leadership is collaborative, the researcher may test this hypothesis by conducting member checks (see Chapter 7) with people in the setting who have served as data sources—as well as those who have not directly contributed data—or by having a peer debriefer analyze the data and challenge the hypothesis or by any other approach he or she may think to utilize.

Respondents can assist the researcher in data analysis and thereby effectively communicate the constructed realities on which they are operating. One particularly useful tool for this is the use of respondents' metaphors. Skipper (1989) asked students, teachers, and the principal to identify metaphors that described their high school. These metaphors caught in an uncanny way the constructed realities that the respondents had been unable to describe directly. Exploring these metaphors with the respondents enabled the researcher to begin to comprehend and share in some of these realities.

Writing is a fundamental analytic activity, and it is particularly critical in linking data analysis at the research site with data analysis away from the site. During her study of diabetic patients, Mobley (1992) painstakingly made entries in three different notebooks. One notebook contained the transcriptions of the diabetes education classes attended by the patients and the notes she had taken during her observations of the classes. From these notes she developed a profile of each patient. In a second notebook she transcribed the tape records of her interviews, after first placing them in the context described in her first notebook. A third notebook served as a journal of her reflections and attitudes and of new questions that were stimulated. Such ongoing analysis not only gave her a growing understanding that systematically enriched the study, but also gave her new direction for her subsequent observations and interviews.

Between periods of data collection and at the conclusion of data collection, analysis enables the formation of a gestalt from the seemingly isolated descriptions provided as well as from those that seem to have naturally emerged together. According to Lincoln and Guba (1985, p. 333), "Data analysis involves taking constructions gathered from the context and reconstructing them into meaningful wholes." This process has three elements: (1) unitizing data, (2) emergent category designation, and (3) negative case analysis. A fourth element is added to analysis that is done between periods of data collection: (4) bridging, extending, and surfacing data.

Unitizing data may be defined as disaggregating data into the smallest pieces of information that may stand alone as independent thoughts in the absence of additional information other than a broad understanding of the context. This does not mean that the whole will be adequately understood when one reads a single unit. A unit of data is said to exist when there is but one idea found in a portion of content. A unit may consist of a few words, a complete sentence, several sentences, or an entire paragraph. The unit must also be heuristic; that is, it is aimed at understanding some aspect of the context or some action the inquirer needs to take (Lincoln & Guba, 1985). Within these limits (i.e., one idea, yet heuristic) the unit should also be the smallest piece of information that can stand alone. As the units are determined, the researcher codes them so that they may be readily accessed as part of the audit trail.

Pennartz (1989) describes the process by which he unitized data taken from transcribed interviews for purposes of applying semiotics to the analysis of perceptions of the urban environment:

> As for selection of fragments from the texts, I applied two criteria. The first criterion was whether or not a fragment contained a sign or sign vehicle as well as an interpretant and whether or not it referred implicitly or explicitly to the experience of pleasantness as an affective response. The second criterion concerned the exactness of the given information. (p. 237)

He provides an example:

> If those shops weren't there . . . and you can imagine those facades . . . they have something personal and friendly about them. . . . (Why do you think of these facades as friendly?) Well, I mentioned this one and that one with the small bay-window . . . . Thinking of the bay-window I imagined sitting there very pleasantly for a while and watching everything pass by. (p. 238)

He uses the example to illustrate his procedure for interpretation of the text:

> Thinking of the bay-window I imagined sitting there . . .
> [another complete fragment]: very pleasantly and watching everything pass by . . .
> [text contains a sign (the small bay-window), an affective response (friendly) and an interpretant (sitting pleasantly and watching everything pass by).] (p. 238)

Emergent category designation involves taking all of the units of data and sorting them into categories of ideas. This allows categories of thought characteristic of a particular setting to emerge intuitively as the researcher's own background and latent theory interact with these data. The categories that emerge should be considered as one analyst's organization of the data. It is possible that no other scholar would discover the same categories. The researcher must understand that the construction that emerges through this practice is but one of many possible constructions of reality (Lincoln & Guba, 1985). This technique consists of the following steps:

1. *Read the first unit of data.* Set it aside as the first entry in the first category.

2. *Read the second unit.* If its content has the same tacit feel as the first unit, then add it to the same pile as the first. If not, then set it aside as the first entry in the second category.

3. *Proceed in this fashion until all units have been assigned to categories.* Units that neither appear to fit into any category nor justify the creation of a new category may be placed into a miscellaneous stack. Understand that these data do not constitute "junk"; rather, they are data that constitute a portion of the environment that the researcher would not likely have discovered had he or she not gone into the context for the inquiry. This "miscellaneous" category will be looked back through later to determine whether data included should be reassigned to one of the other categories or assigned to a new category because of a common theme in the "miscellaneous" category. They may also be dealt with as a whole and included together in the final case report or later discarded because of their inability to provide additional information to the study.

4. *Develop category titles or descriptive sentences or both that distinguish each category from the others.* Write these on separate cards or sheets of paper to mark the categories. These are not set in concrete; they should serve as tentative decision rules for inclusion in or exclusion from the various categories for each piece of datum.

5. *Start over.* Use the cards or sheets bearing the title or descriptive sentence as markers for each category. Spread these out around the work area to serve as bases for the categories. Begin with the first card of the first category and repeat the process that has already been followed. This important step enables the researcher to further focus the content of each category. It is vital that the researcher not confine him- or herself to the

original categories. One must allow new categories to emerge and old categories to dissipate as empty sets. It is probable that the researcher will move cards from one category to another in this step. This step should be no less emergent than the first. The researcher is as free at this point as he or she was initially to place units wherever they seem best to belong. This process may be repeated as frequently as the data warrant.

The process described above is almost as simple as it sounds. The difficulty that arises is determining what to do with a unit of data that could justifiably be placed into more than one category. The researcher should then refer to the tentative decision rules provided by the descriptive sentence or title for each category. If the unit of data could still fit into more than one category, it is up to the researcher to determine whether the unit makes a sufficient contribution to more than one category to justify its inclusion in more than one category. Because the meaning of the data is determined by the context in which they are found, it is very possible that a single unit may make very important and different contributions to two or more categories. However, the researcher must be very careful about putting a unit into more than one category. To put every unit into every category would obviously destroy the value of categorization completely. To put them into categories where they make marginal contributions to category meaning generally serves to weaken analysis.

In his study, Hodson (1991) noted the following:

> After each interview, I transcribed the interview verbatim and filed its material according to the categorization then in use. The material was typically in the form of paragraphs [that] were cross-classified to several categories. As I filed each statement, I compared it with previous statements in that category and kept running notes on the content of each category. The categories changed over time; some disappeared and were merged under more general titles. Some emerged out of previous categories that became too heterogeneous. Some categories became parts of matched pairs or triads. . . . For example, comments [that] described instances of lax work or bad workmanship also typically mentioned abusive management. . . . This helped to reveal connections between categories. (p. 51)

Notice how this categorization process parallels the formation and function of language. Like language, it enables alternative constructions that the naturalistic researcher may consider as he or she seeks to construct realties that are compatible and consistent with those that have been constructed by persons in the setting being studied. This reconstruction process lays the foundation for establishing the credibility of the study.

Given the emphasis in this book on the importance of context, the reader is advised that it is generally best to keep the units of data as close as possible to their original context. Consider the following example from the interview excerpt below (Allen, 1990):

> Robert believes in giving kids as many chances as possible. . . . He's an innovative principal. Any idea you come up with, he's willing to let you try it. He has a lot of patience, which can be a drawback when it comes to discipline. (p. 79)

In this example, the researcher broke each of the four sentences into units of data based on the fact that they represent independent thoughts. The categories that emerged in this study included "Principal Robert Green," "Discipline," and several others. The first sentence in the excerpt was judged to fit best in the category of Principal Robert Green. The second and third sentences also seemed to fit easily and exclusively in the same category. The final sentence of the excerpt posed a problem: It fit both the categories Principal Robert Green and Discipline. Given that the context of the questionable unit was a description of the principal, it was decided to include the sentence with its immediate antecedent in order for the context to assist in interpretation of the unit's meaning. This brings up the point that it is extremely important that the researcher be guided by context. The ellipsis that follows the first sentence in the excerpt indicates that the units naturally appearing between the sentence and the next in the excerpt fit best in other categories and appear elsewhere in the case report.

On the other hand, the following statement made by Principal Green about discipline might be classified differently: "The main problem is these people who are 'off-campus'; they're supposed to have gone and they haven't gone" (Allen, 1990, pp. 120-121). This is a fairly straightforward presentation of a discipline problem, and the information it contains could have probably been obtained through written records or from other persons without shifts in meaning. It tells more about the category of Discipline than it does about the category of Principal Robert Green and should probably be classified as such.

Another statement by Principal Green (Allen, 1990) that tells us something potentially significant about Discipline and Principal Robert Green could conceivably be classified under either category or even in both:

> I get irritated a lot of times when I find a guy who I know has B lunch and
> has been let out of his fifth-period class to go to the restroom one minute
> into fifth period. There is no reason in the world for that kind of thing to
> happen. (p. 120)

Negative case analysis involves addressing and considering alternative interpretations of the data, particularly noting pieces of data that would tend to refute the researcher's reconstructions of reality. Hypotheses are tested against individual pieces of data to determine the viability of the hypotheses. Hypotheses are revised until there are no substantive differences in understanding between the hypotheses and the data. It is unlikely that there will be 100% agreement between hypotheses and all data, because individual perspectives may provide discrepant reports of phenomena, just as one eyewitness may report that an assailant was clean-shaven while another may report that he was bearded.

The consideration of negative cases is an extremely productive tool for analysis. During data collection the naturalistic researcher should be attuned to alternative interpretations of respondents and, if probing indicates that an interpretation has substance, should encourage the respondent to explicate and extend it into a full-blown negative case. Peer reviewers can do the same thing. Also, the researcher's own divergent ruminations about "What if . . . ?" questions can make a similar contribution. Consideration of negative cases should stretch the hypotheses that are being formed. Every opportunity for significant stretching of a working hypothesis can significantly improve and strengthen it.

One approach to negative case analysis that may be useful is similar to an approach used in courts of law: the dissenting (or minority) opinion. If, after careful review and member checking, the researcher is convinced that the picture he or she has drawn is accurate but several persons, or even one key stakeholder, in the context disagree with the picture as drawn, then the researcher may wish to work with the disagreeing parties to develop narrative that provides an alternate interpretation. The other parties may wish to write a response to be included with the researcher's report (Allen, 1990) or may want the researcher to provide an alternate interpretation that represents a different view. Under the assumption of multiple realities, the researcher should not underestimate the importance of negative case analysis. In fact, the researcher should feel comfortable including such reports as dissenting opinion, given that this reflects the complexity inherent in the setting's context and that it enhances the opportunity for thick description (see Chapter 7).

Emergent category designation and negative case analysis focus the search for data in the next round of data collection by the processes of *bridging, extending, and surfacing data* (Guba & Lincoln, 1981). Bridging is appropriate when the researcher notices that two or more categories or two or more separate pieces of data logically suggest a link between them that was not specifically identified by earlier data collection efforts. The "missing link" hypothesis provides direction for the researcher when interviews, observations, and other data collection procedures are resumed. Extending is called for when an emergent category appears to be viable but seems incomplete. Attempts to supplement the data in this category guide further data collection. Surfacing may be used when analysis has defined tentative boundaries for the context being studied and suggests that unexplored, potentially rich sources of data exist within those boundaries that may be tapped in the next round of data collection.

The Interactive Process: An Illustration

The interactive process between data collection and data analysis can be illustrated by the daily procedures followed by one of the authors more than 20 years ago in writing a series of case studies on the principalship. Although time has passed and technology can greatly facilitate the researcher's procedures, the interactive process between data collection and analysis has remained essentially the same.

To write the case studies, the researcher first found it necessary to identify situations that would illustrate the various facets of the principal's job in leading an organization that was dedicated to the education of society's youth within the context of a bureaucratic institution and a dynamic society. Leads to the various situations that provided the basis for the case studies came from a variety of sources: newspaper articles, radio and television reports, contacts in professional associations, and conversations with school principals. After receiving a lead, the researcher would contact additional people in the setting and obtain additional media reports, if available, in order to determine whether the situation offered a suitable setting for the purposes of the proposed case study. After determining that the setting and situation were suitable, he would establish appointments with people in the setting who appeared from his preliminary information to be key informants for the case study.

These initial appointment times were usually set over a three-day period (a limitation set by the researcher's schedule) when the researcher would move to the setting. Initial appointments were ordinarily limited to an hour and were set far enough apart over the three-day period to enable the researcher to establish time for follow-up appointments, make appointments with additional individuals, make observations in the school and community, and obtain copies of pertinent documents and records, including local media reports.

Each night following his data collection, the researcher would summarize all of his data on 3×5 cards, each card containing what seemed intuitively to represent a single item, incident, or interaction. Lengthy documents and records were briefly summarized on one major reference card, with key elements being recorded on separate cards. Following this process, he began separating the cards into separate piles, following an intuitive feeling for how they might be grouped. After grouping all the cards into piles, he would look at each pile separately, giving a label to that group and summarizing in writing the central ideas that seemed to emanate from the cards contained in it. When this was finished, he would review the group labels and then characterize the system he had used to group the cards. He would follow this by projecting an alternative classification system and would distribute the cards according to a new set of groups. He would then repeat the process of reviewing the piles for central ideas and then follow this by projecting yet another classification system. This process continued either until he could not project a new classification system or until he was too tired to continue (the two cutoff points were remarkably synchronous). The final step for the evening was to review plans for the next day in light of the new analysis: Whom else should he see? Whom should he visit again? What different questions should he ask? What else should he observe? What additional documents and records should he obtain? These plans were again reviewed at breakfast the next morning.

Back at home the researcher would make another review of his data and attempt a first draft of the case study. He would force this draft through, even though at many points he felt his information was woefully inadequate. This process inevitably revealed key points in the emerging case that needed further investigation: (1) missing data, (2) competing interpretations, and (3) inadequately supported facts. However, this forced analysis essentially established the agenda for his next visit to the field site: whom he needed to see, what he needed to find out, additional observations he needed to make, and additional documents and records he needed to obtain. This process of alternating between field site and home base would continue as long as was necessary to gather the necessary data for the case study. Subsequent field visits (usually two or three visits after the initial one) were generally shorter than the first one and were always more specific in their pursuit of data. An additional visit was also made, of course, for the final member check, which will be discussed in Chapter 7.

The Hermeneutic-Dialectic Process

Many of the elements displayed in this illustration of the interactive process are parallel to elements of the hermeneutic-dialectic process described by Guba and Lincoln (1989). They describe this process as *hermeneutic* because it is interpretive in character and *dialectic* because it seeks a Hegelian synthesis through comparison and contrast of divergent views. As Guba and Lincoln point out: "[T]he major purpose of this process is not to justify one's own construction or to attack the weakness of the constructions offered by others, but to form a connection between them that allows their mutual exploration by all parties" (p. 149).

As Guba and Lincoln describe the process, the researcher typically starts with one respondent, who is selected for convenience or any other salient reason, and elicits the constructions that this individual has about the entity being described or evaluated. At the end of the interview, the respondent is requested to identify another respondent who has divergent constructions from his or her own. Prior to interviewing the second respondent, the researcher reviews his or her member-checked and analyzed notes to prepare for the interview. Initially, this interview allows the second respondent the same freedom of expression accorded to the first respondent. However, when the second respondent adds no further information, the interviewer introduces themes from the first respondent and asks the second respondent to respond to them. Finally, a nomination for a third respondent is solicited.

The process of interviewing, analyzing, and identifying new respondents continues until information becomes redundant or until it falls into two or more construction categories that remain at odds with each other. As the research proceeds, the basis for successive selection of respondents shifts. At first the purpose is to maximize the range of divergent constructions. As the process continues, the major purpose is to ensure that as many stakeholding groups as possible have had the opportunity to contribute their constructions.

After the first interviews have been completed, another round of interviews is conducted with either the same or a similar set of respondents.

(The total set of respondents responding to the constructions of other respondents is termed a *circle* by Guba and Lincoln.) If the same respondents are used, the early respondents will receive their first chance to respond to the constructions of others in the circle. However, whether the same circle of respondents or a circle of similar respondents is used for this second cycle, the impact of the process is both educative and empowering to those who participate in it, enriching their constructions by bringing them into contact with divergent ones. In addition, other inputs, from outside sources, including other groups of stakeholders and documents, are introduced to the circle by the researcher at appropriate times. Finally, the researcher's own constructions may be introduced and treated to the same degree of criticism, integration, or expansion that the members of the circle have afforded to other constructions.

Using the Microcomputer as a Data Analysis Tool

In conducting a naturalistic inquiry 20 years ago, one would naturally have used note cards and a pen to record data. The note cards would then be sorted according to emergent category technique. Although that method is just as effective now as it was then—and there are many researchers who still adhere to that method—it is no less natural now to use the microcomputer as a tool in dealing with collected data. At the time this text was going to press, numerous qualitative data analysis software packages that were compatible with most computer systems were emerging. The authors strongly recommend that the interested reader refer to Tesch (1990) for a discussion of qualitative data analysis software packages.

In conducting their research on child abuse, Dingwall, Eekelaar, and Murray (1983) had collected data from observations, interviews, and other means that produced more than 7,000 sheets of notes that contained approximately 2 million words. Without computer assistance, the efficient analysis of such a mountain of data would have been impossible. They describe the procedures they followed:

> Analyzing such a volume of material presents its own problems. We adopted a computerized retrieval system. The basic principle is similar to that of indexing a book. A preliminary list of topics is drawn up and each sheet of data given a unique reference number. Every page is then read and coded for the topics appearing on it. In this process further topics may be added, although it is generally advisable to wait until a substantial body of data

has been collected and an extended provisional list created so that the number of topics introduced during coding is restricted. In this study, the initial coding was divided between Topsy Murray and John Eekelaar, while Robert Dingwall checked every sheet. The code sheets are punched and the computer program used to invert them, producing a list of all the locations at which each topic appears. The topics may be connected by various logical operators for sub-searches. We then took the index and used it to make the thematic searches by hand [that] form the basis of our subsequent discussions. (pp. 22-23)

Each author of this book has utilized the microcomputer to some extent as a tool in processing data obtained in naturalistic inquiries. We will present here the approach utilized by one of the authors in his data analysis (Allen, 1990). Any word processing package or database management system may be used in this approach.

Allen (1990) conducted a study of principal-teacher interactions in urban high schools. His primary method of data collection was an individual interview approach with faculty members at two high schools. Interviews were tape recorded, and the researcher attempted to record all he could with pen and paper during the interview. Within two days after the individual interviews, the researcher transcribed the handwritten notes and tape-recorded interviews onto the computer's hard disk. Each interview was stored as a separate document. Once the information was entered onto the computer, the task of unitizing data for use in an emergent category technique remained.

Allen proceeded with data analysis by carefully reading through each complete interview individually as it appeared on the computer screen. As new data were considered to constitute separate units, the researcher separated the units by inserting a hard page break at the conclusion of an individual unit. The software package was configured to provide page numbers and an identifying header for each page. When printed, each page contained one unit of data, identifying information for tracking the data back to their source (via the header), and a page number. One interview that would normally have required 12 sheets of paper for printing would then require as many as 100 or more sheets. The documents were printed, and emergent category technique was employed in sorting through the sheets of data. The identifying headers and page numbers served as important tools in easily identifying sources and contexts as needed. It also provided the backbone for the audit trail.

Jackson (1992) used a computer software package, Ethnograph (Seidel, Kjolseth, & Seymour, 1988), to analyze the data he collected from his interviews with older custodial and landscape workers. Jackson entered the verbatim transcript of each interview into Ethnograph, which prepared the transcript for coding by arranging it on the left-hand side of the page. With this printout in hand, he categorized the data according to an emergent classification system. Once coded he was able to retrieve the information either by single category or by combinations of categories. Each grouping or combination of groupings would support alternative and extended interpretations of the data and thereby enrich the analysis process. The process was not essentially different from that described earlier, in which one of the authors arranged 3×5 cards according to alternative classification systems. However, computer technology, as Jackson used it, may greatly facilitate the process by which alternative classification schemes (and resulting alternative interpretations) can be viewed and integrated with each other in the analysis process.

Group Data Analysis

Analysis can be strengthened considerably by increasing the number of competent analysts who are involved in the process. The advantage gained need not be simply a linear one. Each analyst should not simply add an incremental piece of knowledge; rather, the process should be an interactive one in which the different orientations of the different analysts are reflected in the respective analyses that can be used to stimulate and challenge the analyses of others and be resolved in a new, more fertile understanding of what the data mean.

One format for group analysis is the data-based debate proposed by McNamara, Fetsco, and Barona (1986). The procedure was used by Witters-Churchill (1988) in her study of how Texas principals perceived their preparation programs. To analyze responses to two open-ended questions, she assembled two 4-member panels of professors and students of educational administration. One team was the primary classification group for one of the two open-ended questions; the other group was the primary classification group for the other open-ended question. Each team became a challenge group for the question for which it had not provided primary classification.

The teams created a classification scheme for the responses to each of the two questions. First, members of each team recorded on 3×5 cards the separate responses to one of the questions. Next, each team broke into groups of two and sorted the cards into categories of responses that appeared to arise. The full teams reconvened and shared their proposed classification schemes. Members were instructed to question the proposed schemes in two ways: (1) Are the proposed categories the best groupings of the responses? (2) Are the individual responses placed in the correct categories? This process was continued until consensus among the members of each team was achieved. The identical process was repeated by each team using the question for which it was the challenge group.

After the teams completed their primary classification systems, they prepared a formal presentation and defense of their proposals. Next, the teams prepared a challenge to question the classification system of the opposing team. Finally, the teams met for a formal two-hour debate. During the debate, each team presented its system, followed by a challenge by the other team and a presentation of the opposing system, which in turn was followed by a final defense by the classification team. The process was repeated for the second question. After the debate, the teams reconvened and modified their original classifications using the information they gained from the challenge group. Their final products provided valuable material for Witters-Churchill as she used them to challenge her independent analysis and create a more fertile final analysis for her study.

A similar procedure was used by Wilmore (1988) in her study to identify criteria for judging the performance of principals. Two panels of principals, made up of professionals with outstanding reputations from widely separated geographical locations across the nation, first individually, then as separate panels, and finally, in a debate between the two panels at a common meeting point, identified the criteria that were being intuitively used by practicing principals to judge job performance in a variety of field settings.

There is, no doubt, an endless variety of specific procedures that might be used to obtain the benefits of group analysis; but these two brief examples illustrate several of the pieces that should be part of any group analysis. First, it is important that the persons chosen to participate in the analysis be competent to analyze the data. Simply using individuals who lack either experience or sophistication will not enrich the analysis. Second, each analyst should first make an independent analysis so that he or she can make an independent contribution to the group analysis. Finally, a second level of debate between groups that have already synthesized individual views should be added to the process. Though this may not always be possible, as it was in these two examples, this second-level group debate adds considerable strength and fertility to the entire analysis.

Triangulated Hypothesis Testing

Another approach to utilizing a variety of perspectives in looking at data collected was used by one of the authors in his study of the high school principalship (Allen, 1990). In this approach, the researcher gave individual portions of unedited data (usually complete transcripts of individual interviews) to a wide variety of educators for their review and interpretation. The participants in this phase of analysis included public school teachers, university professors, and graduate students in a variety of education-related disciplines. Persons involved with the research project were not included in this phase of analysis, because it was feared that their independent knowledge of the whole would affect their interpretation of the part they were assigned. The task at hand for each participant was simple: He or she was asked to read the interview transcript or set of observations given and to write a brief description of the school based solely on what had been read. Given that the interviews and sets of observations ranged from very brief to quite lengthy, the reviewers had varying degrees of difficulty in drawing inferences about the whole based on their specific parts. The participants did not communicate with one another or with anyone else familiar with the study as they performed the task at hand. What emerged from this set of independent reviews and interpolations was remarkable: In only one case did a reviewer provide a description of the school that was not compatible with the constructions generated by the researcher's own prior analysis. That particular negative case was based on an interview that had already been interpreted as divergent from other perspectives provided by respondents. The uncanny resemblance between the individual descriptions of the parts submitted and their similarity to the interpretation of the whole, made independently by the researcher, served to add great confidence to the researcher's belief that he had arrived at a reasonable understanding of the school being studied.

Summary

A central feature of naturalistic research is that analysis is continuous and that the analysis of data interacts with the collection of data. This occurs in many ways. Subsequent interviews are shaped by what has been learned from previous ones; a single interview may change course in midstream because of what has been learned during the interview. New opportunities for data collection are seized as the researcher's learning clarifies the data's significance. Multiple working hypotheses are tested continuously. All of this is possible through the wonderful biological computer that is built into the human instrument. In addition to operating during data collection, sustained intense data analysis occurs between periods of data collection and at the conclusion of data collection. Subsequent periods of data collection are informed by what the researcher has learned through analysis of data that have been previously collected. Analysis is never really complete, and, even in the first report of a study, competing interpretations of the data are likely to be included. Analysis is a rich, broad, wonderful activity that, perhaps more than any other aspect of naturalistic research, celebrates the link between the researcher and the setting being studied.

For Further Study

1. Again consider the data that you collected in Chapter 5 (For Further Study Questions 2 and 3). Design alternative categorization schemes for these data and use these categories to write at least two alternative case scenarios (3 to 5 pages each).

2. Examine again the studies you reviewed in Chapter 5 (Question 1). Describe the analysis processes that were used in these studies. Clarify how data analysis interacted with data collection.

3. Again consider the plans you have been laying for a naturalistic study since Chapter 1. What plans can you make at this point to ensure that the data collection and data analysis processes are interactive? Can you build the benefits of group data analysis into your plans? Build these proposed procedures into your ongoing plan.

7

Quality Criteria for a Naturalistic Study

WE WILL NOW examine the standards by which a naturalistic study may be properly judged. In this examination we will return first to the need for establishing trustworthiness that was introduced in Chapter 2. Steps for establishing trustworthiness must be planned as the study has begun and developed as it unfolds; the final product must communicate to its audience that the study is worthy of this attention. In fact, the naturalistic researcher must be especially concerned with the issue of trustworthiness because it is in this area that he or she is most often attacked with charges of "sloppy" research and "subjective" observations. A major purpose of this chapter is to help the naturalistic researcher know and be able to apply the techniques that establish each aspect of naturalistic inquiry's trustworthiness. In addition, the authors have found that in writing and presenting such research it is helpful to have a thorough understanding of how the aspects of a naturalistic inquiry compare to conventional scientific inquiry.

Establishing trustworthiness enables a naturalistic study to make a reasonable claim to methodological soundness. In doing so, the naturalistic researcher is able to answer many of the attacks of traditional researchers and is usually able to satisfy most neutral observers that naturalistic methodology provides an equivalent basis for being seriously considered. However, because of the naturalistic researcher's paradigmatic assumptions, this is not sufficient. Probably of greater importance are criteria that are not merely parallel to those required by the traditional paradigm but that spring from the naturalistic paradigm itself. The naturalistic paradigm, valuing as it does the separate realities that have been created by individuals, must also value the way these realities are responded to and the ways in which they enable individuals to respond productively to their environments. Guba and Lincoln (1989) have identified the standards by which this responsiveness to multiple realities is judged as authenticity criteria.

Finally, for the same internal reasons that compel the authenticity criteria, ethics in research is not a cumbersome "add-on" to naturalistic inquiry, but a logical outcome of the paradigm. Because the paradigm deals in the constructions created by the stakeholders in the context being studied, they must be honored and protected from negative effects of the research. The purpose of naturalistic inquiry is to understand the constructions of the respondents on their own terms. The study that damages or destroys the constructed realities in the context of its study in effect destroys itself.

How Is Trustworthiness Established?

Trustworthiness is established in a naturalistic inquiry by the use of techniques that provide truth value through credibility, applicability through transferability, consistency through dependability, and neutrality through confirmability. The techniques and their relationship to traditional inquiry are summarized in Table 7.1 (adapted from Lincoln & Guba, 1985). The techniques listed were introduced in Chapter 2.

The student in a conventional research class quickly learns that trustworthiness in such a study is provided through the techniques that give truth value through internal validity (for example, control and randomization), applicability through external validity (for example, randomized sampling), consistency through reliability (for example, odd-even correlation of test items, test-retest or parallel forms correlation), and neutrality through objectivity (for example, intersubject agreement). In a naturalistic inquiry, alternative techniques to support truth value, applicability, consistency, and neutrality have been developed.

Naturalistic Techniques That Provide Trustworthiness

Prolonged Engagement

The first of the techniques that help establish the truth value or credibility of a naturalistic inquiry is *prolonged engagement*. Prolonged engage-

Table 7.1 Establishing Trustworthiness: A Comparison of Conventional and Naturalistic Inquiry

Criterion	Conventional Term	Naturalistic Term	Naturalistic Techniques
Truth value	Internal validity	Credibility	Prolonged engagement Persistent observation Triangulation Referential adequacy Peer debriefing Member checks Reflexive journal
Applicability	External validity	Transferability	Thick description Purposive sampling Reflexive journal
Consistency	Reliability	Dependability	Dependability audit Reflexive journal
Neutrality	Objectivity	Confirmability	Confirmability audit Reflexive journal

Adapted from Lincoln & Guba, 1985.

ment provides a foundation for credibility by enabling the researcher to learn the culture of an organization or other social setting over an extended time period that tempers distortions introduced by particular events or by the newness of researchers and respondents to each other's presence. Prolonged engagement also helps the researcher build trust and develop a rapport with the respondents.

Distortions may be caused by the events that occur within a particular time span. The month before the closing of public school at the end of a spring semester is a very atypical one. Schedules are busier; organizational routines are more intense; school professionals are under greater pressure. The researcher who observes only this month in the school's life learns the culture of the school through very distorted lenses. On the other hand, if the researcher's study excludes this period, important keys to understanding the culture may be lost.

Distortions to the research may be introduced by the respondents or the investigator and may be unintended or intended. Distortions may include personal biases of the researcher that favor a particular organizational management style or a particular teaching style. Distortions also occur simply because of the attention given to individuals during the research, attention that may cause them to act or react differently. For example, when a principal observes a class, teachers often comment that the students acted better (or worse) than usual.

In addition, distortions may be caused by respondents wanting to please the investigator, presenting their own personal inclinations, wanting to deceive or confuse the researcher, or not wanting to respond at all. Moreover, distortions can be flagrantly introduced by a respondent who has a hidden agenda. In the Skipper (1989) research, in response to the interview question "What is the worst thing that has happened to you while at this school?" two interviewees reported extremely negative information regarding a district administrator. This was a distortion that was propagated by a small group of individuals who had a hidden agenda of trying to discredit the individual and thus reduce the individual's power. This distortion served to point the research in the wrong direction, and much time was spent investigating the charges that proved to be false. Through prolonged engagement and continued data gathering, this information was appropriately investigated. The researcher must constantly be on the watch for such misinformation introduced deliberately or inadvertently by respondents. Lightfoot (1983, p. 370) stated that in qualitative research "the person" is the research tool, the perceiver, the selector, the interpreter, and the guard against distortions of bias and prejudice. Lightfoot also said that "investigators should be aware of the biases that plague their perceptions and try to counter those by the pursuit of contrary evidence." In addition, she said that the researcher "listens and accepts, but is not controlled, enhanced, or diminished by others' perceptions or judgments" (p. 377).

Prolonged engagement also serves to build trust and develop a rapport with the respondents. For instance, in the Skipper (1989) study, the researcher was a new member of the organization and perceived by the respondents to be an ally of the new superintendent who had hired her. During her research she distanced herself from the superintendent by not carpooling to work with him or eating lunch with him. In addition, she ate lunch in the teachers' lunchroom each day. She also conducted the data analysis over a seven-month period of time. During this time, trust developed as the respondents saw that the superintendent's interests were not being served, confidentiality was being honored, and the respondents were having input into the inquiry process. However, trust is fragile, and the researcher must be extremely careful, for one mistake can instantly destroy trust.

In his study, Fleisher (1989) says that he began to earn respect:

> . . . by participating in every correctional activity, particularly in 'emer-gencies'—fights, assaults, stickings, escapes, and a killing. Responding to emergencies was the most significant aspect of my daily participation in the penitentiary, of building rapport, and of understanding violence as it affects inmates and staffers alike. . . . But it wasn't until after my participation in a serious assault in 1985 that I began to see the positive social effects of getting involved in violence. Afterwards, staffers reacted to me differently than they had before. Staffers who hadn't said anything to me before this . . . now began paying attention to me. . . . I felt a sense of belonging to the group. (pp. 108-109)

Johnson (1975, p. 111) states that field researchers agree on the "critical importance of personal relationships involving trust for gathering data in social research." He also says that there is a common consensus among researchers that being honest, being open, and being a "nice guy" are in some manner related to the validity of data collected during a field investigation. In addition, he says that trust can be developed by the researcher showing that he or she can organize data to provide a rational account of the social order, by showing that he or she has an interest in the research observations and cares about the persons in the research setting, and by operational procedures that are guided by the principle of "fitting in." In other words, the investigator strives to maintain the integrity of the persons and situations encountered by minimizing social distance and using middle-of-the-road strategies.

Johnson (1975, p. 142) cautions that in some research relationships "sufficient trust" replaces trust. He defines "sufficient trust" as "a personal, common-sense judgment about what is accomplishable with a given person." He sensibly says that there is a realistic limit to what a mother of four in her 50s will tell a 29-year-old doctoral candidate at a local university.

A caution to prolonged engagement must be given. Lincoln and Guba (1985) caution against what anthropologists call "going native." This is a condition evidenced by the researcher becoming so much like the group he or she is studying that he or she ceases to be a researcher and in fact loses research perspective. Lincoln and Guba (1985, p. 304) state that tendencies to go native are abetted by prolonged engagement.

Fleisher (1989) found himself going native after many months of sub-mersion in the penitentiary. It became increasingly difficult to keep his thoughts separate from those of the staff and inmates, and as this occurred, he lost touch with his role as a research anthropologist and began to think of himself as a correctional worker. His research agenda began to become indistinguishable from his thoughts and ideas as an insider. Notions, opin-ions, and beliefs of inmates and staffers blended with his own. He took on the values of the staffers, managers, and administrators with whom he worked and socialized. He defended the prison system to his friends and neighbors and became increasingly aggressive with impolite convicts. He became his own informant and answered his research questions based on his own experience and insights. As he recognized that this was happen-ing, he turned to his academic colleagues for help in regaining his perspective. With their assistance he believes he was able to do so.

In a review of Fleisher's research (Jacobs, 1991) states that even after Fleisher consulted with his colleagues at the academy, he doubts that he succeeded in regaining his objectivity. Jacobs states (1991, p. 115), "From this point on in the book, I feel his attempt to describe the life of 'staffers, inmates, and executive administrators *from their perspectives'* (emphasis added) is badly biased." Jacobs goes on to say that what troubles him most is that while this is a commendable ethnography of prison life, some segments are probably distorted because of the above reasons; as a result, the recommendations for improving prisons are not supported by the data.

Lightfoot (1983) says that even those researchers whose forays are brief are usually aware of the interventionist quality of their work, including the ways in which they have disturbed the environment. The advantage of a short stay would be that the researcher would not be in the system long enough to impact social change; however, the briefness prohibits the amount of time needed to build rapport and trust. While a longer stay invites more intrusive interaction between the researcher and the participants in the system, at the same time it provides the opportunity to build the relation-ships needed to obtain in-depth, accurate data.

Persistent Observation

While prolonged engagement serves to temper distortion caused by the researcher's presence, persistent observation accentuates that presence by actively seeking out sources of data identified by the researcher's own emergent design. Persistent observation according to Lincoln and Guba (1985, p. 304) adds salience to a study that otherwise might appear to be no more than a mindless immersion. They also say, "If prolonged engagement provides scope, persistent observation provides depth."

Lightfoot (1983) refers to persistent observation as dependent on the researcher's ability to seize the moment and take personal risks. It is not passive; it contains a strong sense of purposefulness and assertiveness on the part of the researcher. She found that the people rose to the occasion, responded with intensity and thoughtfulness, and appreciated the focused attention. Lightfoot adds that this skill was particularly important to her because she had a relatively short time to spend in the field in each of her studies.

Persistent observation helps the researcher sort out relevancies from irrelevancies and determine when the atypical case is important. For instance, in the Skipper (1989) study, the students in a high school on a U.S. Air Force base were often described as competitive and independent, yet in one interview a teacher related that the students were so dependent on the base exchange that they would not have paper if the base exchange was out of paper. Another teacher said that the students were fearful of walking along a river on a school outing and physically hung onto one of the chaperons. At first this information may have seemed irrelevant or atypical, but on further investigation, it became apparent that the students were competitive and independent and able to assimilate quickly within their protected environment marked by the chain link fence of the base. Outside the base it was sometimes a different story. Without persistent observation, the earlier hypothesis would have been retained. According to Lightfoot (1983, pp. 13-14), "the truth lies in the integration of various perspectives rather than in the choice of one as dominant and 'objective'; . . . I must always listen for the truth . . . not disregard it as outside the central pattern."

For these same reasons, it is important to avoid premature closure of an investigation. Such closure may result from funding problems, demands of clients, an intolerance for ambiguity, or a desire to complete the task. In any case, the inquirer may embrace one interpretation too soon that is likely to result in an inappropriate hypothesis. Lincoln and Guba (1985, p. 305) state that "in those situations where lies, fronts, or deceptions are being practiced, early closure makes it especially easy to pull off such deceits."

Triangulation

Triangulation leads to credibility by using different or multiple sources of data (time, space, person), methods (observations, interviews, videotapes, photographs, documents), investigators (single or multiple), or theory (single versus multiple perspectives of analysis) (Denzin, 1970).

If a study focused on the reactions and interactions in a hospital regarding the death of patients, the sources of data could be different times of day (morning, midday, midnight), different wings of the hospital (pediatrics, obstetrics-gynecology, intensive care), and different role groups (doctors, nurses, volunteers, relatives). Methodological triangulation can take many forms, but it will usually be the combination of two or more different research strategies. In the hospital example, the researcher might begin by asking nurses in the particular hospital how they react to the death of a patient. This information could be triangulated by the researcher making observations of nurses' reactions to death. Doctors or relatives may be interviewed or surveyed regarding nurses' reactions to death. Artifacts such as memos, diaries, anecdotal records, and absentee reports could also be part of the triangulation process. Between-method triangulation (observations, interviews, documents) is favored over within-method triangulation (observation A, observation B, observation C).

According to Lincoln and Guba (1989), each piece of information in the study should be expanded by at least one other source, such as a second interview or a second method. Single items of information contribute little to an understanding of the context of the study unless they are enriched through triangulation. In addition, the absence of information can also provide important information. For instance, in the Skipper (1989) study the principal stated, "I talk one-to-one rather than through memos." This statement was triangulated not only by interviews with teachers and observations but also by the absence of any such memos in the files.

Investigator triangulation simply means that multiple as opposed to single observers are employed. When multiple observers are used, the most skilled observers must work closest to the data. The "hired-hand" approach is to be avoided. If colleagues report the same kind of observations, confidence in the observations increases (Denzin, 1970). In Chapter 1 of this book a team of five members worked independently and kept their own schedules, yet they came to three convergent conclusions regarding the organization being studied. Lincoln and Guba (1985) suggest that in such a case provisions be made for intrateam communication to keep all members moving together. They also feel that team members are kept "honest" by other team members, thus increasing the probability that the findings will be credible.

Theoretical triangulation is an element that few investigations achieve. It involves the use of several perspectives in the analysis of the same set of data (Zelditch, 1970). For instance, in the hospital example, it may be found that the data gathered by the researcher could be screened by the motivation theories of Maslow or Herzberg, thereby expanding the constructions built on that data. The example in Chapter 4 of one of the authors whose data described a Likert System 4 organization, although he had not been looking for it, could be considered an example of theoretical triangulation.

The degree of convergence attained through triangulation suggests a standard for evaluating naturalistic studies. In other words, the greater the convergence attained through the triangulation of multiple data sources, methods, investigators, or theories, the greater the confidence in the observed findings. The convergence attained in this manner, however, never results in data reduction but in an expansion of meaning through overlapping, compatible constructions emanating from different vantage points.

Referential Adequacy Materials

Referential adequacy materials support credibility by providing context-rich, holistic materials that provide background meaning to support data analysis, interpretations, and audits. These referential adequacy materials may be obtained through both obtrusive and unobtrusive measures. Obtrusive measures are those that tend to intrude to some degree on the environment. These measures include photographing, videotaping, and tape recording done by or for the researcher. Unobtrusive measures include the collection and review of brochures, catalogs, newspapers, yearbooks, photographs, memos, and information in teachers' boxes, all of which are usually obtainable and were originally produced without reference to the researcher. All of these referential adequacy materials help to provide a slice of life that may be invaluable to the researcher in understanding the context of an organization.

There are several strategies and sources that may be particularly useful in establishing referential adequacy in a school environment. First, the researcher should have a box in the teachers' lounge so that he or she receives all communications received by the individuals in the organization, noting what is not there as well as what is there. Second, the researcher should begin taking and gathering photographs and placing them in an album. One researcher found these pictures, as well as those found in the journalism department, useful in analyzing many of the hypotheses that developed. Third, in a high school, the yearbook and newspaper are valuable items. In each yearbook the staff sums up in pictures and short statements the hopes, dreams, and accomplishments of a particular school year. Over time, multiple yearbooks tell a great deal about a school's ongoing culture. Lightfoot (1983, p. 17) notes that such an item is important "in order to get a sense of how the school wanted to be perceived; how it sought to characterize activities and events; and who seemed to be the leading public figures, the most popular symbolic images." Similar strategies and sources can be used to accumulate referential adequacy materials in other environments.

Such materials, though they communicate rich meanings to both the researcher and the study's audience, are not used as a part of the formal analysis. Instead, although collected during the study, they are used after the analysis to support the audit process and to enrich the meanings communicated by the study. Bifano (1987; Bifano & Erlandson, 1989) took numerous still photographs during her dissertation study of three schools. These photographs focused on the physical environment (rather than on people) and, for the most part, captured parallel scenes in the three schools (classrooms, hallways, restrooms, offices, playgrounds, etc.). She did two things with these photographs. First, she asked a group of physicians to look at each set of pictures and give their impressions of the school. Their comments were remarkably compatible with her analysis of the human interaction in each of the three schools. Then at the final defense of her dissertation, she allowed her dissertation committee members to view the photographs and give their impressions of how compatible their portrayal was with the human interactions she had recorded. After they had described the high degree of compatibility they saw, she played the tape-recorded observations of the doctors who had not seen her written record. She used this convergence of constructions to introduce the audit trail for her study.

Peer Debriefing

Peer debriefing helps build credibility by allowing a peer who is a professional outside the context and who has some general understanding of the study to analyze materials, test working hypotheses and emerging designs, and listen to the researcher's ideas and concerns. In such sessions, the researcher thinks aloud and explores various hypotheses, while the peer debriefer asks probing questions, plays devil's advocate, and provides alternative explanations. Such sessions also allow the researcher to vent frustrations and emotions that may cloud the research. The peer debriefer can listen sympathetically to these feelings, defusing as many as possible, and help the inquirer devise coping strategies. This technique is particularly valuable in helping the inquirer deal with a process that is a lonely one.

Fleisher (1989) used peer debriefers who were colleagues in various universities to help him try to regain his objectivity when he became too socialized in the culture of the prison he was studying. He also thought that conversations with them helped him devise his research strategies and organize his thoughts.

The debriefer should be someone who is the inquirer's peer (Lincoln & Guba, 1985). If the debriefer is not a peer of the researcher, dangers exist, such as that the debriefer's inputs may be discarded or considered mandates. Generally, a member of one's doctoral committee should not be the peer debriefer because he or she is in an authority relationship with the researcher. The process may be an informal one using friends or colleagues.

Furthermore, the debriefing session should include a discussion of the emerging methodological design, and a written reflective paper for the audit trail should be prepared at the end of each session. The paper should summarize the issues, the concerns, the emerging hypotheses, and the emerging design for documentation purposes.

During the course of her study of diabetic patients, Mobley (1992) selected as her primary peer debriefer a woman who was a dentist and also happened to be a diabetic who had been through diabetes education. As Mobley shared her observations and the perceptions and feelings of the clients with her peer debriefer, this professional was able to help her interpret what she saw and heard and determine if her data were typical for diabetic patients or were more likely to be generated by other factors, such as the client's socioeconomic status. After her study, she identified another peer debriefer, a national expert in the field of diabetes education, to read her report, challenge her conclusions, and suggest alternative interpretations.

With regard to peer debriefing, the researcher must be aware that he or she has relationships both with members in the organization and with professional colleagues (Johnson, 1975). The researcher must be able to move back and forth between these two simultaneous roles. Relationships and conversations with colleagues may serve to keep the research honest, and many ideas for the research will emerge from the contacts. On the other hand, the researcher must remember that colleagues, friends, and family members are the ones who shower or withhold statements of praise or encouragement. Whether one stays with the project or not often depends on them. They can have a great deal of influence on the research, its direction, and what gets reported. How does this affect the gathering, analysis, and reporting of data? The researcher must be on guard because one's personal feelings become fused with the relational endeavors of the project through these necessary human relationships. Naturalistic researchers must be true to the context and its members. As stated in Chapter 2, in order to do this, naturalistic researchers must learn to step out of themselves so that they can view life through the eyes of the respondents.

Member Checking

Member checking provides for credibility by allowing members of stakeholding groups to test categories, interpretations, and conclusions. According to Lincoln and Guba (1985) this technique is the most important in establishing credibility. It is in this step that the members of the setting being studied have a chance to indicate whether the reconstructions of the inquirer are recognizable.

Do not confuse member checking with triangulation, a process that is carried out with data from one source checked with data from other sources. Member checking is carried out in regard to the constructions from the triangulated data.

Member checking is conducted continuously and is both formal and informal. Listed below are areas in which member checking is often conducted during a naturalistic inquiry.

1. Member checking may be conducted at the end of an interview by summarizing the data and allowing the respondent to immediately correct errors of fact or challenge interpretations.

2. Member checking may be conducted in interviews by verifying interpretations and data gathered in earlier interviews.

3. Member checking may be conducted in informal conversations with members of the organization.

4. Member checking may be conducted by furnishing copies of various parts of the inquiry report to various stakeholding groups and asking for a written or oral commentary on the contents.

5. Before submission of the final report, a member check should be conducted by furnishing entire copies of the study to a review panel of respondents and other persons in the setting being studied.

Member checking is not as easy as it may seem, particularly with the written report. One of the authors found it difficult to ask system participants to read descriptive passages about themselves or their programs. In preparing to ask the principal to read a descriptive passage about himself, the researcher was warned by system participants that although the passage was accurate, the principal might not want to admit to some of the information gathered through teacher interviews. However, when the principal finally returned it and said he thought it was accurate, it was easier for the researcher to submit other segments for review.

The researcher must be prepared for a variety of reactions as members of the organization review "the black-and-white" interpretations of their cultures. Lightfoot (1983) reports a headmaster who, in reading a naturalistic inquiry on his high school, said part of the pain experienced in reading the report reflected the discomforts associated with uncovering the truths.

There are dangers that exist in the member-checking process. Some systems do not support criticism. As reports for one author came back from high school faculty and staff with no remarks or suggestions for improvement, it soon became evident through a peer debriefing session that perhaps a working mode existed in the school organization that did not support criticism or constructive feedback. A further analysis of the system found that this was indeed the case. As a result, the member-checking process was limited to a few individuals who would be critical and honest rather than put harmony above all. The researcher found that high school students were extremely helpful in providing straightforward member checks and overcoming the problem described.

Another danger is that member checks can be misleading if all the members share some common myth or conspire to mislead. According to Lincoln and Guba (1985), if an investigator is taken in, it is an easy next step for the member checks to verify the validity of what has been "found." The human instrument must be on guard.

The Reflexive Journal

The reflexive journal supports not only the credibility but also the transferability, dependability, and confirmability of the study. According to Lincoln and Guba (1985), a reflexive journal is a kind of diary in which the investigator on a regular basis records information about him- or herself. The journal provides information about the researcher's schedule and logistics, insights, and reasons for methodological decisions. Lincoln and Guba suggest a daily journal, but it takes a great deal of discipline at the end of a day to make entries in such a journal. Some researchers have found it easier and more practical to word process entries in the journal on a weekly basis. The printout of the journal subsequently becomes a part of the audit trail for the study.

Excerpts from one author's (Skipper, 1989) reflexive journal follow:

An October entry

During this time, I really get to know the students and their parents, teachers, and principal. I find the students assertively polite in accomplishing their goals—particularly the seniors as they strive for scholarships .... The teachers continue to be friendly, and accept me totally. I have been with them enough that I have been able to see individual flaws. Some appear too structured for the kind of school we have with a constantly changing student body. . . . Due to the requirements of my job, I will not begin the formal interview process until November. That will probably delay my second round of interviews until January; however, I think that will be workable.

A November entry

Time is getting away from me regarding the interviews partly because I am on campus only half of the time. At least now I have the questions ready. The questions were selected to get background information on the interviewees, to use Herzberg's questions to learn the outer bounds of experiences, and to obtain information on the communication patterns and possible metaphors to address my research questions.

A December entry

The interviews have gone much better than I expected. The teachers seem happy to have someone listen to their views on the school. . . . I was concerned about the metaphors until after I had gotten some from students. They have been great! It will be hard to pick one as THE metaphor. I probably will blend several together. After the principal gives me his metaphor, I am going to have him read and respond to the others.

A January entry

I interviewed the principal today. The interview was not as productive as I had hoped even though it lasted over 2 hours. He deals with specific questions better than open-ended questions; therefore, I will use more of them in the future to get the information that I need from him.

A February entry

This week I commented to the principal that I think I would have been better to come in, do the study, then leave on a short timeline. I have been here too long. I am beginning to see through the teachers. I must be careful in using the word "dedicated." It applies to some but certainly not to others. For many, what I had originally mistaken for dedication is perhaps better described as a looking out for oneself and doing what it takes to stay in what is certainly an ideal teaching situation. . . . I am making lists of questions that need to be answered. I then identify and question people who can answer them.

A March entry

After interviewing the students last week, I have modified my hypothesis about the division of students based on their Dad's rank (Officer vs NCO). One student called it an "imaginary" difference since students who wanted to could easily cross over the line. Also, as one teacher said, the students who have trouble would have trouble anywhere. The modification checked out with others. . . . I am closing out my work quickly due to organizational and possible personnel changes that may affect me and my role in the school.

The keeping of a reflexive journal, while serving a different purpose, need not be a separate activity from those activities associated with data collection and analysis. Fleisher (1989, p. 103), at the end of each day in the penitentiary, organized his notes and updated his contact log (a list of inmates and staffers—where they spoke, what they talked about, and for how long). He also began categorizing his interview data such as: "New Hacks (training problems; family troubles; personal history; work experience, etc.); . . . Rapport (was I doing well? how did I know that?); Questions (whom will I talk to next? about what?); Networks (who introduced me to whom? how are they connected?); and so on." Armed with questions, he began the next daily round.

Thick Description

Thick description provides for transferability by describing in multiple low-level abstractions the data base from which transferability judgments may be made by potential appliers. Lincoln and Guba (1985, p. 125) state that "The description must specify everything that a reader may need to know in order to understand the findings (findings are NOT part of the thick description, although they must be interpreted in the terms of the factors thickly described). . . . "

To be sure that one will have the data necessary to write the thick description, it is important to be very aware of the context, using *all* of the senses. While in the context, it is important to stop and look, listen, smell, and feel the surroundings and interaction. When reading a description, one should be able to get a feel for what it is like to actually be in the context. The following excerpt is from Lightfoot's *The Good High School* (1983, p. 157):

> Inside, the smell of years of chalk dust sifted down between the planks of wood floors reminds me that I am in school. . . . As I walk through the halls—with light brown and golden-colored bricks, institutional green and pale blue walls, low ceilings, and narrow walkways—it feels as if I am walking back in time. . . . Brookline High is comfortable and old feeling—free of the modern sleek lines, open spaces, and bright lights of many modern school structures.

In this passage the reader, through the many descriptions, is able to begin visualizing Brookline High School. In writing such descriptive passages, some researchers find it helpful to pull up a chair in the context and begin taking notes. From that vantage point, what can be seen, heard, smelled, and felt? In taking notes and writing such passages, the writer should be careful to see the forest and the trees. For example, one author sat in front of a high school and took copious notes for descriptive purposes, only to return home and find that nowhere in the notes was the color of the school's bricks recorded.

Fleisher (1989) includes the following thick description in his study:

> I visited Eddie in his cell on a Wednesday night in September 1986. He, Cowboy, and several other inmates were busy collecting money to make a special commissary purchase that evening. Eddie was sitting on his plywood toilet-bowl cover, counting money that Cowboy was gathering from inmates along the cell-range. They were all getting excited about going to the commissary. Eddie said he was buying four six-packs of canned orange juice that he, as a self-proclaimed master prison winemaker, was going to ferment into a "delicious sweet, orange wine tonight," he said, "for a Friday night blowout." (p. 121)

A physical description of the site is much easier to write than descriptions of people. Descriptions of people must not come across as caricatures. In dealing with a descriptive passage of a high school principal, which had the potential of becoming a caricature, one researcher involved two teachers in the school to help write the description. The first attempts were comical. The description below was the final version (Skipper, 1989):

> He is described by the teachers as "conservative," "clean-cut," and "honest." One person summed it up by describing him as a "Country Gentleman." This description is reinforced by his "western-cut clothes" and eelskin boots. He is above average height with sandy brown hair that is described as "never having a hair out of place." He is noticeably trim, the result of dieting that relies on avoiding the homemade cinnamon rolls and tempting lunches made in the school cafeteria. Noted for a "hearty" laugh, a good sense of humor, and blushing easily, he is "young looking" for his nearly 50 years. (p. 50)

In writing descriptive passages such as this, it is helpful to use quotes from the interviews of people in the context so that the reader as well as the researcher can analyze the data. Descriptions of interactions, such as that in the example below, will also be part of the thick description.

> Within classrooms, students appear to be treated with unusual fairness. Their individual dimensions are noticed and responded to by teachers while their group identification seems to fade away. Although students within classrooms seem to receive evenly distributed and unbiased attention, the difference between the levels of instruction at Kennedy are vivid. Honor students have a dramatically different school experience than the remedial students. Faculty describe the contrasts as the difference "between night and day, black and white, not even in the same ball park." (Lightfoot, 1983, p. 85)

According to Lincoln and Guba (1985, p. 316), what constitutes appropriate thick description is still not completely resolved. Not all descriptive data will do; and "the criteria that separate the relevant from the irrelevant descriptors are still largely undefined." However, to offset the problem, Lincoln and Guba suggest that the inquirer provide the widest possible range of information for inclusion in the thick description through purposive sampling.

Purposive Sampling

As we noted in Chapter 5, naturalistic inquiry relies on purposive sampling rather than on the techniques of random sampling usually seen in the conventional paradigm. Purposive sampling requires a procedure that is governed by emerging insights about what is relevant to the study based on the focus determined by the problem and purposively seeks both the typical and divergent data to maximize the range of information obtained about the context. According to Lincoln and Guba (1985, p. 210), "The object of the game is not to focus on the similarities that can be developed into generalizations, but to detail the many specifics that give the context its unique flavor. A second purpose is to generate the information upon which the emergent design and grounded theory can be based."

According to Lincoln and Guba (1985), maximum variation sampling is selected in ways that provide the broadest range of information possible. It does not suppress the deviant case and allows for the uncovering of a full array of multiple realities. The procedures of purposive sampling depend on emergent design rather than a priori design. The decision to stop the sampling process is made when redundancy of information occurs, not when a statistical confidence level is reached.

One of the authors began purposive sampling by asking the principal of the high school being studied to identify faculty members and students who might be considered typical cases (Skipper, 1989). This group became the initial group in the purposive sample. Consistent with the naturalistic inquiry design, a problem was *not* identified by the researcher before the interviews. Unstructured, exploratory interview guides that also explored the parameters (highs and lows) of experiences were used. One question was "Tell me about Randolph High School." Another was "Think of a time you felt exceptionally good (or bad) being here at Randolph High School." At the end of each interview, the researcher also asked "Whom else do I need to speak to in order to learn about Randolph High School?" and "Who might have a different view of Randolph High School?" It was through these questions that an individual was located who knew the long-forgotten but important history of the school. Interviewees continued to be selected to allow the researcher to fill in the gaps and focus on insights until the point of redundancy of information was reached.

The Audit Trail

The audit trail leads to dependability and confirmability by allowing an auditor to determine the trustworthiness of the study. It is important that adequate records be kept during the study. Lincoln and Guba (1985, pp. 319-320) give six categories of audit trail materials: (1) raw data (interview guides, notes, documents), (2) data reduction and analysis products (3×5 cards, peer debriefing notes), (3) data reconstruction and synthesis products (grounded theory and data analysis sheets, reports), (4) process notes (journal), (5) materials relating to intentions and dispositions (inquiry proposal, journal, peer debriefing notes), and (6) information relative to any instrument development.

Schwandt and Halpern (1988) have developed a four-stage model for planning, organizing, recording, and delivering an audit trail. Planning includes determining whether an audit is desirable, how the audit will be structured, what will be included in it, and how it will be prepared and maintained. Organizing has to do with the determination of what records will be kept (audit trail substance) and how they will be filed (audit trail structure). Recording refers to the establishment of a well-organized system of records and files both to improve the quality of the inquiry as it unfolds and to enable review of the study's quality after the fact. Delivering means providing the auditor with access to the audit trail at an appropriate time.

Schwandt and Halpern give considerable further direction for the implementation of this model. They recommend a record-keeping system for the audit trail that provides for a thick description of both the inquiry context and the inquiry process. They also recommend that both substantive items (inquiry plans, events under study, an account of the researcher's decisions and actions, and an account of the researcher's thoughts and feelings) and structural considerations (a filing system, cross-references, indexes, and dates) be built into the audit trail as it is established. They suggest six types of files for the audit trail: three that represent the phenomena being studied and three that represent the procedures of the inquiry.

The files representing the phenomena being studied include raw data files, data reduction files, and data reconstruction files. Raw data files contain the totality of information from which findings are derived. They include notes acquired from observations, interviews, documents, and other sources. Because they are the closest that the auditor will get to the context being studied, the credibility of the study in the auditor's eyes will be strongly influenced by them. They will include both data that have been filtered through the researcher and those that are relatively unfiltered (actual quotations or tape recordings) and both low- and high-inference data as classified by where they are on the abstraction ladder (as described in Chapter 2) and the amount of their interaction with the researcher's own constructions. Times and dates on the raw data records will facilitate both an audit and the study itself. Data reduction files include (1) condensations of notes to facilitate communication, (2) write-ups that are made to clarify data soon after they have been acquired, (3) categories that have emerged to classify unitized data, (4) visual displays to summarize large quantities of data, and (5) any computer analysis summaries that have been used to manage large amounts of data. Data reconstruction files track themes as they emerge from the raw data files and data reduction files to form overall themes for the study. They include (1) theoretical notes that represent new constructions and working hypotheses as they emerge during the study, (2) visual displays that show the relationships among categories, (3) findings and conclusions that are logically related to the categories of data that have been identified and examined, and (4) reports (whether interim or final) that have been made of the study.

The audit trail files representing inquiry procedures include notes about the process of the inquiry, notes about intentions and motivations, and copies of instruments, tools, and resources. Process notes include methodological notes that provide information about how procedures, strategies, and day-to-day decisions were adopted or made during the study. They also include trustworthiness notes—which track the steps that were taken to enhance credibility, dependability, and confirmability—and audit trail notes, which provide a road map into the audit trail. Files about intentions and motivations include the original inquiry proposal (to enable the auditor to assess the interaction between the original framework of the study and emerging needs); personal notes that reveal the feelings, introspections, fears, biases, and emerging values of the researcher during the study; and a record of the researcher's thought processes as they developed and as they guided the inquiry. Finally, the audit trail files should provide the auditor with the key questions that guided the inquiry (both initially and during the process), the preliminary interview protocols that were used, the various tools that were used to collect data, and the tools that were used to analyze data.

The key to the audit trail is reporting no "fact" without noting its source and making no assertions without supporting data. One researcher found that the audit can be facilitated by cross-referencing the final report by means of an outline with the raw data and data reduction products (Skipper, 1989). An assessment of the study can be facilitated by identifying a part of the thick description in the final report, finding it on the outline that accompanies the study (which is facilitated by page numbers), and referring to the note cards, photographs, or artifacts indicated on the outline.

To further facilitate this process, the note cards in her study were marked "IA," "IB," "IE1," "IE2," and so on to show where in the outlines, and thus in the narrative, the information was reported. Photographs were simply numbered. The artifacts were coded "B" for Air Force base information, "S" for school information, "C" for school calendar information, "A" for school annuals, and "N" for school newspaper articles. Table 7.2 presents a portion of the audit trail that was used in this naturalistic study, showing how information was triangulated.

Enabling Authenticity

As important as it is, trustworthiness is not sufficient as a measure of quality in a naturalistic study. Nor is it even paramount. Trustworthiness speaks to methodological adequacy; by establishing it, the naturalistic researcher can make strong claims to methodological safeguards that parallel those established by traditional researchers. But the naturalistic paradigm demands more. Unlike traditional inquiry, which believes in a single objective reality, naturalistic inquiry takes its strength from the separate realities that have been constructed by different individuals. These separate realities must be given status in the lives of those individuals, in the contexts in which they operate, and in reports of inquiry (Guba & Lincoln, 1989). The award of such status is recognized as "authenticity." It is the duty of the naturalistic researcher to enable it.

Methodological adequacy is not sufficient because it cannot by itself guarantee that these basic tenets of the naturalistic paradigm will be served. Consider, for example, the implications of two strategies for establishing trustworthiness: prolonged engagement and persistent observation. By enabling contextual understanding that maximizes the advantages of both native and outside observer, the researcher acquires enormous power for affecting processes and outcomes in the setting being studied. That power can be used wisely or unwisely. To this point in our logical trace, most traditional researchers would agreed with us. They would also agree with us that power should be used wisely, though most would agree that this is not always done.

The two paradigms diverge when we seek to determine what is meant by "wisely." The traditional researcher would rely on such criteria as "accepted practice," "previous research," or "legitimate authority." The naturalistic researcher would not deny any of these but would also demand that they be brought into a hermeneutic dialectic (see Chapter 6) with the constructions of the various stakeholders in the social contexts. This is paramount in research that honors these constructions and recognizes that any common movement among the stakeholders depends on the development of shared constructions to which the separate constructions have contributed.

Table 7.2 The Audit Trail

Randolph High School Stability Within Transition

	Index Card	Photos	Artifacts B: Base D: District S: School C: Calendar A: Annuals N: Newspaper
I. A Rich History (p. 44)			
A. Location of the base/the TAJ	IA, IB	4, 5, 6	B1
B. Base description/access	IB	6	B1
C. Base housing description	IB, IC		
D. History of the base		B1, D2	
E. Mission of the base/Education of personnel	IE(1-3)		A(1, 2), D2, P32
F. History of the school district/funding	IF(1-2)		N(34, 35, 41)
II. The High School (p. 47)			
A. Perimeter Road			
1. Description	IIA	7	
2. Stadium	8, 9		
3. Trees	8		
B. Campus description	IIB(1-2)	10, 11, 14, 80, 81	A(1-5, 12)
C. High school office description/secretaries	IIC(1-6)	65, 66	
D. Teachers' lounge description		67, 68	
E. Patio area description	IIE	15-18, 24-28	
F. Main classroom building description/display cases	IIF	30-44, 49	
III. The Principal—"Do what's best for the kid!" (p. 51)			
A. Physical description		2, 90	
1. "Conservative"	IIIA2(1-2)	2, 90	
2. "Clean-cut"	IIIA2(1)		
3. "Honest"	IIIA2(2), IIIA3		
4. "Country Gentleman"	IIIA4		
5. "Western-cut clothes"	IIIA4	2, 90	
6. "Never having a hair out of place"	IIIA2(1)	2, 90	A16
7. "Trim"	IIIA6(1-2)	90, 92	

Excerpted from Skinner 1989.

Fairness is the first authenticity criterion. The constructions of all stakeholders must have equal access to the process by which group direction is determined. Guba and Lincoln (1989) state that "the role of the evaluator is to seek out, and communicate, all such constructions and to explicate the ways in which such constructions—and their underlying value systems—are in conflict" (p. 246). It is the job of the researcher first to identify all stakeholders and to solicit their within-group constructions. The researcher must also work to achieve an open access by which these constructions are shared (between stakeholding groups and the researcher) and conclusions, recommendations, and action steps are determined. Fairness also demands a continuing open process that provides an appeal mechanism for stakeholders who believe that the process has been compromised.

Informed consent obtained at the beginning of the research must be renewed continuously because the human context and the power relationships within it continuously shift. A formal agreement that gives the researcher access to conduct research within a social context is a meaningless document if the realities of that context have shifted in a way that makes stakeholders perceive the research as inimical to their interests. The researcher who insists that the original formal agreement be honored in such a case is asking to engage in a counterproductive activity. The open process on which the research depends has been effectively closed, and no formal agreement can open it. The continuing renewal of informed consent, of course, makes the researcher extremely vulnerable.

Such vulnerability is anathema to the traditional researcher who believes that procedures for a study and matters of access must be determined in advance. How can a researcher guarantee validity, reliability, or objectivity if he or she is not in control of the research process? The experienced naturalistic researcher recognizes, however, that such vulnerability, rather than being a liability, is actually an asset in conducting the research. Consider, for example, the case of one of the authors, described in Chapter 4, who worked with the principal and faculty of a new urban high school in the first year of its operation. The agreement between principal and professor was, from the beginning, very open and very general. Both believed that the trade-off (of access to data in exchange for feedback and recommendations) was a fair one that would benefit both parties. Both knew tacitly that if either party was not satisfied with the arrangement at any point, then the agreement would be abandoned. Because the researcher assumed that a suitable understanding of the school and its procedures could only be obtained through the dialectic interaction of the various stakeholders' constructions with each other's and with his own, the researcher used the process to identify data and develop stakeholder constructions that could genuinely be used in the operation of the school. The principal, for his part, recognizing that he was obtaining very useful feedback from the researcher, took care to see that the researcher's access to data was not curtailed. Both parties took strength from fulfilling what they saw to be the mutual benefits they had envisioned in their original very loose and informal contract. Every day brought about a renewal and specification of this contract, which not only was a liberating experience for the researcher, but also accomplished much more than could have been specified in a formal contract at the beginning of the process.

Ontological authenticity, the second criterion, derives from the expansion of the constructions that individuals bring to the social context, enabling them to improve the ways in which they experience the world around them. This criterion can be demonstrated through the testimony of individual respondents that they have in fact enhanced their understanding and through recorded observations that mark the expansion of their constructions.

Educative authenticity refers to the extent to which respondents' understanding of and appreciation for the constructions of other stakeholding groups has expanded. This criterion can be determined from the testimony of the respondents or from observations of their growth through the dialectic process.

Catalytic authenticity represents the extent to which decisions and action are facilitated by the expanded constructions of the stakeholders. To determine if this criterion has been reached, we may consider the demonstration of willingness of respondents to use their expanded constructions as a basis for action, the actual decisions that emerge from their learning in the research process, and observed actions and changes over a subsequent time period.

Finally, there is *tactical authenticity*. This criterion refers to the degree to which stakeholders are empowered to act. Their willingness to make decisions, develop plans, or even take action is meaningless if these decisions, plans, or actions have no potential for impact on the shape and future of the social context in which they operate. Tactical authenticity can be determined by testimony of stakeholders, follow-up observations of the ways in which stakeholders participate in the context, and demonstration of empowerment during the research process itself.

Ethical Considerations

The same paradigmatic features that demand the criteria of authenticity for naturalistic research also shape the way in which the naturalistic researcher considers the ethical obligations of his or her inquiry. Unlike the traditional researcher, for whom ethical considerations often seem a necessary burden that must be attended to if the research is to go forward to accomplish more noble ends, the naturalistic researcher proactively initiates ethical standards into the research process because they are the essence of what research is all about and can only enhance it.

Conventional research views a code of ethics as a series of safeguards to protect subjects (and the "subject" label tells much about the conventional stance) from the research. First, the subject must be protected against physical or psychological harm, including loss of dignity, loss of autonomy, and loss of self-esteem. Second, the subject's privacy and confidentiality are protected. Third, the subject is protected against unjustifiable deception. Finally, before the research can take place, the subject must give informed consent to participate in it.

The naturalistic researcher provides these safeguards for his or her respondents in ways that go well beyond those envisioned or even possible under the prevailing paradigm. *Harm* is a term that the naturalistic researcher seeks to make more inclusive in order to proactively protect respondents. *Privacy* and *confidentiality* are confined not only to what the researcher disseminates but also to necessary personal space that the researcher declares off-limits even to his or her own investigation. *Deception* is never justified, not only because it is at a minimum demeaning to the individual who is deceived but also because it is counterproductive to the researcher's open and free exchange of constructions among stakeholders and between the researcher and the respondent. *Informed consent*, as discussed in the preceding section on authenticity, cannot be entirely achieved at the beginning of the study, even if it is the intent of the researcher to do so, because the research context is constantly in flux and neither researcher nor anyone else really knows what is being consented to. Also, many traditional researchers would consider fully informing subjects about their intended procedures as potentially compromising their research. By contrast, the naturalistic researcher, as we saw in our earlier example, welcomes the opportunity to daily renegotiate and expand the basis for informed consent as new opportunities for collaborative activity emerge.

Safeguarding respondents against harm is not well served by any checklist or formula for resolving ethical questions. The naturalistic researcher is likely to face a multiplicity of unanticipated ethical dilemmas. In such situations we would encourage the researcher always to go back to the premises of the naturalistic paradigm and proceed with the sensitivity and integrity that it mandates. Situations parallel to those that are likely to be encountered in a naturalistic study have been described by several researchers.

In his study of a prison system, Fleisher (1989) says that because some staffers and inmates were in highly sensitive situations, if their names or nicknames were revealed their personal safety or careers in the institution would be jeopardized. Even with their consent to use their names, he chose to use pseudonyms and omit potentially damaging or identifiable information from their accounts. In addition, he made the decision to not disguise his role or his purpose in the organization. Whether participant observation in a disguised role is ethical has been the source of much discussion. Some researchers (Denzin, 1970) believe that it is ethical as long as there is no damage to the credibility or reputation of the subject and the integrity and anonymity of those studied (unless otherwise directed) are maintained. We believe with Lincoln (1990) that such deception is subversive to the research effort and counterproductive to the search for the multiple social constructions that individuals hold.

Lidz (1991) noted the particular problems that arose in his role as an "observing participant" in a study of difficulties and satisfactions experienced by Jewish spouses in Jewish-Christian families. He noted:

As a member who seeks also to be a methodical observer, one encounters a "chronic" issue of obtaining and maintaining informed consent for adding research about the group to the other dimensions of personal participation. If it is accepted that one is member first, observer second, the right to be an active observer is less identified with one's participation and hence prone to being made problematic. There are likely to be actual or potential stresses on the group arising from one's endeavor to broaden the personal role to accommodate observation. The researcher should be prepared to discuss these stresses frankly with the group not only before obtaining its permission to conduct research, but also on a recurring basis. One should be prepared to give up the research or even resign from the group if one loses legitimation for one's inquiry. It is especially important to address other participants' worries that one may harbor secret agendas for the group or may wish to see through or unmask others. . . . When I assured the group that neither exploration in the modes of depth psychology nor unmasking of hidden motives would be involved in my study, although I did hope to learn the specific concerns and interests of all of the members as individuals, worries over the role that I might play appeared to evaporate quickly. Yet, I found that this assurance had to be renewed on a few occasions and its basis in sociological methods explained again. (p. 84)

Smith (1990) shares an incident that occurred during his NIE-funded field research in a school district. Throughout the project, he made every effort to keep the site of his soon-to-be-published work anonymous. As he concluded his work, the district became entangled in a widely publicized desegregation lawsuit. Because he knew more about the history of the school district than anyone else, the district lawyer wanted him to testify as an expert witness. Such testimony would reveal the name of the district and the school and in effect violate all commitments to maintain the anonymity of the participants. At the same time, refusing a subpoena left him with the possibility of a fine or a prison sentence. He discussed the issue with colleagues in his department, university lawyers, and district administrators. To the superintendent, the issue was simple: "You can't violate your commitments to the staff, teachers, and administrators of Kensington. We'll solve our court problems without involving you." (Smith, 1990, p. 271)

In contracted research there might come into play issues regarding parameters that restrict freedom, the suppression of negative findings, limited distribution of results, and the contractor's "right to know" confidential information (Soltis, 1990). In addition, how will the results be used? Honest, critical research may result in the loss of public funding. Pressure groups demand to have their viewpoint explicated. As a result, external funding, contracts, and potential political outcomes make research, both qualitative and quantitative, ethically complex. On the other hand, the methods used to provide construction fidelity in qualitative research serve to prevent some of the larger abuses often associated with external funding (Lincoln, 1990). In addition, graduate students conducting naturalistic research must guard against endorsing positions that they believe are more pleasing to dissertation committee members.

Federal mandates have attempted to enforce ethical considerations in all research performed at universities. Although these regulations originally covered only federally funded research, they have been expanded to include all research, whether funded or not, at any institution receiving federal monies. As Murphy and Johannsen (1990) have observed, the regulations of an institutional review board (IRB) are not designed to meet the complexities of ethnographic or other nontraditional research and may be used by those who oppose or do not understand it to plant roadblocks in its way. Nevertheless, because ethical considerations are paramount in the planning and implementation of the naturalistic researcher, the intent of the federal mandates is quite welcome and is not seen as an irrelevant intrusions. The naturalistic researcher, by remaining true to the principles of developing a true partnership with the study's respondents and of negotiating outcomes prior to reporting them, will easily exceed the federal requirements. Often he or she can use the IRB's procedural requirements to communicate to colleagues in the university both the strong ethical stance that is taken by naturalistic research and its efficacy in answering significant questions.

As a researcher explores an organization, it is possible that he or she may learn of illegal activities. Johnson (1975, p. 165) says it is "inconceivable to me to report such actions to the legal authorities." He cites his belief in the confidentiality of the research information as the reason. He concedes that not everyone agrees with this viewpoint. The researcher has mixed obligations. He or she must either break confidence and lose research opportunities or maintain confidentiality and let the authorities handle things. In school settings the problems can involve the selling of drugs; in welfare organizations, it can involve misappropriation of funds; in political arenas, it can involve breaking into offices to obtain confidential information (e.g., Watergate). There is no simple solution or one answer to these ethical dilemmas. The researcher must decide what is appropriate considering his or her values, the public worth of the research, and the complexity, depth, and impact of the illegal activity.

However, while naturalistic researchers are, by the implications of their own paradigm, eager to safeguard their respondents, their view of the ethical dimensions is much more comprehensive and proactive. Participation in a naturalistic study by a respondent should not only not be demeaning, but also not be a neutral experience. The naturalistic researcher, rather than acquiring power or supporting existing power structures, seeks to *empower* all who participate in the study. Each individual's constructions are openly solicited and honored and provided with access to the development of shared constructions.

Participation in a naturalistic study should also be *educative*. Opportunities to share, confront, criticize, and learn from one another's constructions is a central feature of naturalistic inquiry. Each participant emerges with more information and better understanding than he or she or she had initially. Accountability is jointly developed among the individuals and stakeholding groups and is jointly monitored as decisions are developed from shared constructions.

Finally, participation in a naturalistic study promotes *connection* by developing shared constructions among the stakeholders and with external referents. Such connection blunts the need for justification of separate positions and enables participants to jointly reach richer levels of understanding and insight.

The naturalistic ethical considerations of empowerment, education, and connection (Guba & Lincoln, 1989) were demonstrated to some degree in the previous example, provided in our discussion of the fairness criterion, of the author who worked from a loose informal agreement with the principal of a new urban high school to use data obtained from the school's stakeholders to learn about the operation of the high school and the people in it and to use that learning to support the operation of the school. As he interacted with faculty, students, and parents (as groups and individuals), he used his growing understanding (gained from his access to the constructions of many stakeholders) to educate, connect, and empower. As a link between the various stakeholding groups and to resources from outside the school, he was able to help them expand the constructions that they used to order their daily activity. He also helped them expand their understanding and insight regarding each other's constructions by relaying what he had observed and acquired from other groups. In addition, he listened to them as they shared their dreams about the school and worked with them and identified resources to support those dreams. A letter written to the researcher's dean by the principal at the end of the school year describes these impacts, noting that the first year had been one of growth, success, and empowerment—effects that he generously traced to the conduct of the researcher in interacting with the school's stakeholders (R. R. Mastruzzi, personal communication, 10 May 1973).

Similar ethical dimensions were also demonstrated in the dissertation study of Sandra L. Bifano (1987). Her intensive work and interaction with the principals and faculty of three elementary schools clearly resulted in relationships with each of the three principals that educated and connected them. All three found that her study enhanced their understanding both of their own positions and styles and also of their faculties' views and expectations. All three found that the study provided them with productive alternatives for future interactions with their faculties.

Final Thoughts on Quality

Trustworthiness is a matter of concern to the consumer of the report who will use the research for thought or action. According to Lincoln and Guba (1985), the credibility criterion is considered the most important aspect of establishing the trustworthiness of a study to the consumer. A naturalistic inquiry exists in an open system and therefore is never unassailable. The inquirer must come to terms with skepticism and doubt that can never be totally dismissed. The probability that the findings and interpretations of a naturalistic study will be found to be credible depends on the inquirer's demonstrating a prolonged period of engagement, providing evidence of persistent observation, triangulating sources and methods, conducting extensive member checks, and guarding against both going native and premature closing. The novice researcher considering a naturalistic study should see that, despite the absence of correctional studies and levels of confidence, a naturalistic inquiry is as much of a challenge and can establish trustworthiness at least as well as a conventional study. Table 7.3 summarizes the techniques for establishing trustworthiness.

But the naturalistic paradigm requires its adherents to go well beyond methods that parallel the efforts of traditional researchers. Because the traditional paradigm considers research as something done from the outside, only the needs of external audiences (the external research consumer, critics, and the researcher him- or herself) need be considered. But the naturalistic researcher, having intruded on the social context being studied and having opened, confronted, and learned from the constructions of that context's stakeholders, does not have this luxury. The researcher establishes a partnership with the stakeholders in the study, a partnership that requires a free and honest exchange of the separate constructions of all participants and in return offers opportunity for growth and empowerment. The implementation of the partnership builds authenticity into the research. In the same way it brings the research beyond the conventional safeguards provided by research ethics. It not only promises that respondents will not be deprived of something of value that they had before, but also promises value (in the currency of empowerment, education, and connection) that they did not have before the study.

Table 7.3 Summary of Techniques for Establishing Trustworthiness

Technique	Results	Examples
Prolonged engagement	Build trust Develop rapport Build relationships Obtain wide scope of data Obtain accurate data	Length of time in the field Avoiding premature closing
Persistent observation	Obtain in-depth data Obtain accurate data Sort relevancies from irrelevancies Recognize deceits	Purposeful, assertive investigation
Triangulation	Verify data	Using different or multiple sources (interview notes, videotapes, photos, and documents), methods, or investigators Absence of data
Referential adequacy	Provide a "slice of life"	Unobtrusive measures such as brochures, catalogs, yearbooks, photos, memos, etc.
Peer debriefing	Test working hypotheses Find alternative explanations Explore emerging design and hypotheses	Formal or informal discussions with a peer
Member checking	Test categories, interpretations, or conclusions (constructions)	Continuous, formal or informal checking of data with stakeholders such as at the end of an interview, review of written passages, or the final report in draft form
Reflexive journal	Document researcher decisions	Daily or weekly written diary
Thick description	Provide data base for transferability judgments Provide a vicarious experience for the reader	Descriptive, relevant data
Purposive sampling	Generate data for emergent design and emerging hypotheses	Maximum variation sampling that provides the broadest range of information based on relevance
Audit trail	Allow auditor to determine trustworthiness of study	Interview guides, notes, documents, notecards, peer debriefing notes, journal, etc.

Adapted from Lincoln & Guba, 1985.

For Further Study

1. Read one of the six descriptions of high schools in Sara Lightfoot's *The Good High School.*

- Discuss from the description her reliance on the senses (sight, hearing, touch, smell) and give examples of each.
- From the reading, what referential adequacy materials would you expect to find in her audit trail? Give examples that support your answers.
- Write a one-page reflective statement about how you felt while reading Lightfoot's description.

2. Form an audit trail, using the assignments and papers written in Chapter 5 (For Further Study Questions 2 and 3) and Chapter 6 (For Further Study Question 1). Outline the study you have conducted and correlate the outline to the note cards, the notes you made on the member check comments, and the analyses you have made. Attach a photograph of the area.

3. Prepare a graph or table to summarize how you will ensure trustworthiness in the study you have been planning since Chapter 1.

8

Preparing the Report

LINCOLN AND GUBA (1985) have recognized the case study as the vehicle of choice for reporting the results of the naturalistic study. According to Borg and Gall (1983), the case study report involves an investigator who makes a detailed examination of a single subject, group, or phenomenon. In the past this approach has often been rejected as unscientific, mainly because of its perceived lack of research controls. As the acceptance of qualitative research methods has increased, the use of participant observers has revived the case study approach. The case study should not be confused with a narrative, which is much less complex than a case study and is written from one viewpoint.

In this chapter we will focus primarily on the development of the case study as it is used in reporting naturalistic inquiry. It should be kept in mind, though, that there is no single format for reporting such research. In a naturalistic study the principal task of the researcher is to communicate a setting with its complex interrelationships and multiple realities to the intended audience in a way that enables and requires that audiences interact cognitively and emotionally with the setting. Such communication is always a work of art and as such may take many forms. Some of these will be discussed briefly at the end of the chapter.

The Case Study Format

The case study approach has a long history in educational research. In fact, much of the work of Sigmund Freud and Jean Piaget employed case studies. In looking at organizations, the case study approach was used by Theodore Sizer (1984), Sara Lightfoot (1983), Thomas J. Peters and Robert H. Waterman, Jr. (1982), Tracy Kidder (1990), Samuel Freedman (1991), and Mark Fleisher (1989).

The rationale for using the case study mode is that such a report form raises the reader's level of understanding of the focus of the study (Lincoln & Guba, 1985). The format also has the following advantages for the naturalistic inquirer:

- The case study is better suited for *emic* inquiry (a reconstruction of the respondent's constructions), while the conventional report seems better suited for a priori *etic* inquiry.
- The case study builds on the reader's tacit knowledge by presenting holistic and lifelike descriptions that allow the reader to experience the context vicariously.
- The case study, more than the conventional report, allows for the demonstration of the interplay between inquirer and respondents.
- The case study provides the reader an opportunity to probe for internal consistency (factualness and trustworthiness).
- The case study provides the "thick description" necessary for judgments of transferability between the sending and receiving contexts.
- The case study provides a grounded assessment of context by communicating contextual information that is grounded in the particular setting being studied. (Lincoln & Guba, 1985, pp. 359-360)

The case study may be written for the following purposes:

- to record history
- to teach (as in the case studies used in educational psychology)
- to provide vicarious experiences for the reader in the context being described
- to chart future directions of an organization
- to facilitate change
- to revise issues for future consideration.

In addition, the case study may be written at different analytic levels from factual to interpretative to evaluative. Each purpose and analytic level requires different actions from the inquirer and results in a different product.

To complete the case study successfully, the writer must have several characteristics. First, he or she must have above-average writing skills. In many ways, the writing of a case study is more demanding than a technical report or a journal article. It is a lot like writing a novel and requires considerable creative writing ability. Second, the writer must be willing to accept feedback from respondents and use it to develop a better case. The primary object of writing a case study is to write in such a way that the product is credible to the respondents in the context. Another object is to put the reader vicariously in the setting. And lastly, the writer must have actively participated in the research. The knowledge such a person has will be important in organizing the report so that it makes sense.

The report itself is generally written informally in the third person using the natural language of the respondents, and it should be free from jargon. (However, when the researcher him- or herself is involved in the setting being described, it may at times be advisable to use the first person.) As Lincoln and Guba (1985, p. 365) say, the report should see the world "through their eyes." In addition, the writing must be free of the inquirer's interpretations and evaluations in the descriptive segments so that the reader can make his or her own interpretations.

The segment below from Freedman's *Small Victories* (1991) illustrates how the researcher can handle the difficult task of balancing respondents' and researcher's voices:

> At a few minutes before eight, the hall is almost serene, the only sounds the whirl of the duplicating machine, the click of new heels on waxed floors, and the laughter of reacquaintance. One teacher unlocks the sepulchral storage room next to the English office, and out seeps the rich, musty, familiar smell of books, the aroma of *The Pearl*, *Hamlet*, and *Huckleberry Finn*. Despite the broken typewriters in Room 334, despite the shortage of chairs in Room 431, despite the fact that no two clocks tell the same time, all in Seward Park is, more or less, well. Nothing will seem so still and orderly again until July.
>
> Then the moment comes and the doors swing open and the students burst into Seward Park, sending alarms of arrival up stairs and around corners. Before the first face appears on the third floor, Jessica can hear a wall of sound, a compression of sound, massive if indistinct. It reminds her of a bowling alley, with the steady wooden thunder of pins falling. A newcomer might mistake the racket for anarchy, but Jessica, a veteran, welcomes it as the audible expression of possibility, of hope. (p. 23)

The case study contains several parts. First, it has an explanation of the problem or entity being studied. This portion includes a statement of the problem, the significance of the study, research questions, operational definitions, assumptions, and limitations. Second, it contains a review of the literature that helps the researcher and reader view the study in alternative ways. The third section explicates the naturalistic inquiry methodology and includes information on the population, instrumentation, procedures, data analysis, trustworthiness, and audit trail.

The fourth part of the case study is the descriptive portion, which may be similar to one of the segments in Lightfoot's *The Good High School* (1983). Included in this crucial segment would be a description of what the senses detected while in the setting; a description of the transactions and processes observed in the setting; a discussion of the important issues, trends, and patterns that were studied; a discussion and analysis of the working hypotheses that were explored; and a communication of the respondents' constructed realities.

The next part of the case study contains a discussion of the outcomes of the inquiry and may include limitations, conclusions, implications, and ideas for further research. The investigator's credentials, interview questions, survey forms, time lines, computer software packages, and so on would be included as appendixes.

The case study should also have a companion volume that includes items of the audit trail such as original interview notes, actual survey responses, member-checking forms, peer debriefing notes, reflexive journals, photographs, audiotapes, and videotapes. Loose-leaf notebooks work well for many of these items.

Guba and Lincoln (1989) have identified four categories of criteria that a good report should meet:

- *Axiomatic criteria*, by which we mean that the study must resonate with the axiomatic assumptions (the basic belief system) that underlie its guiding paradigm. It must, for example, reflect multiple rather than single realities.

- *Rhetorical criteria*, by which we mean those relating to form and structure, including (following Zeller, 1987) unity, overall organization, simplicity or clarity, and craftsmanship. The latter is characterized in a case study that displays power and elegance, creativity, openness, independence, commitment, courage, and egalitarianism.

- *Action criteria*, by which we mean the ability of the case study to evoke and facilitate action on the part of readers. These criteria include fairness, educativeness, and actionability or empowerment.

- *Application or transferability criteria,* by which we mean the extent to which the case study facilitates the drawing of inferences by the reader which may apply to his or her own context or situation. These criteria include the presence of thick description, provision of vicarious experience, metaphoric power, and personal reconstructability. (p. 224)

Writing the Report

The first step in writing the report is to carefully index the data materials so that they can easily be found as needed in the writing process. One way to coordinate all of the different sources is to extract information from interviews, surveys, audiotapes, videotapes, and artifacts (yearbooks, newspapers, etc.) and place the unitized information on note cards (or their equivalent on paper or computer disk) as described in Chapter 5. Once this is accomplished, only the note cards will be used in the actual writing of the case study. Based on the process described in Chapter 6, the note cards will be sorted into categories or themes from which working hypotheses are explored and developed. The case study will be written to reflect these themes and hypotheses.

The next task is to develop the provisional outline for the case study based on what the inquirer thinks the story line will be. In this outline the inquirer may want to include the following with regard to the context: history of the organization and description of the site, key players, and transactions and interrelationships. The case study outline will be organized around the working hypotheses. This outline should be very detailed and aim for overinclusion of data. Once the provisional outline is completed, it will undergo revision as the case study is generated.

The third task is to cross-reference the indexed materials (note cards) to the provisional outline. The writer will depend on this indexing to locate materials from which to write. One author found it easiest to read each card and determine where it was located on the outline. The researcher then noted on each note card its outline location (IIB1a or IIID2c, etc.) If an item belonged in more than one place on the outline, then it was helpful to make a duplicate of the card. The note cards were then stacked in outline order to facilitate the writing. This process makes it very easy to conduct one last check to ensure that each item is triangulated (are there multiple cards documenting the item?). It also makes it easy to find large segments of data that have been left out of the outline. Moreover, the groundwork for the audit trail as described in Chapter 7 has been laid by this process.

The writer is now ready to begin the actual writing process. The outline is followed carefully; because the cards are now in the same order as the outline, it is relatively easy for ideas to flow together from several sources. Using this process, descriptions may be extracted and direct quotes may be easily found. It is helpful to the reader if subheads, introductory and summary sections, transitions, and logical sequences are used throughout the case study. When difficult passages have to be written, the researcher should consider having respondents in the setting help write those portions of the case study.

Lightfoot (1983) prepared for writing her case studies by reviewing carefully her daily records and summaries, taking notes on her notes, and considering alternative interpretations of her data. Incongruities caused her to look deeper into her data. As similar ideas persistently arose from her data, central themes began to emerge that cut across her study. As the skeleton of each school's story became evident, Lightfoot provided flesh for it with detailed evidence, subtle description, and multiple perspectives. As this task reached accomplishment, she shifted her focus to the aesthetic form of the story she was telling, being careful not to let the momentum of the story distort the data in any way. As a safeguard, she returned often to original notes and relied heavily on direct quotations.

Lightfoot (1983, p. 7) calls her case studies "portraits," because case studies, like portraits, must capture the essence and myriad dimensions of the subject. For the social scientist, this reporting mode must combine both science and art. The case study must capture the organization and its features, characters, values, and rituals. It must also capture the connections between the individual and the institution—how the participants create the culture of the organization and how they are shaped by it. As Lightfoot says, she tells the stories "from the inside out."

As the writer completes portions of the case study, it is important to have members of the various stakeholding groups respond to the descriptions. One of the authors, in completing a case study, attached the following note to each portion of the case study and distributed it to several members of the organization:

> In order to ensure that the context of this study is accurate, I need your help in reviewing the attached description and analysis. Please write on the copy itself, and give any comments or concerns that you may have regarding the accuracy of the materials. Also, if you prefer, we can discuss your concerns. Thanks for your help! (Skipper, 1989)

Some of the comments were: "I don't get this point"; "This gives a rebellious flavor to the paragraph—is that what you meant?"; "What you have is correct, but that wasn't the end of the story"; "Right on! Can I read the rest?"; "You have that this pertains to all students when it should actually be only the seniors."

The writer reviews these comments and makes revisions as appropriate. While it may not be possible to incorporate all suggestions, they must all be taken seriously as outcomes are negotiated. When the redraft is completed, it is again submitted for critique. At this stage, having reviewers comment only on the changed sections saves time.

While both formal and informal member checks have been conducted throughout the project, when the draft is completed it is time to test the credibility of the inquiry report as a whole with the respondents at the site. Reviewers representing all stakeholding groups of the organization(s) should be selected (teachers, administrators, managers, clerks, students, inmates, parents, customers, etc.). Some of these individuals will have been involved in earlier stages of the research. For others, this will be their first exposure to the research. The reviewers should represent diverse perspectives and have spent adequate time in the setting to give a native's view. The reviewers should receive a completed, revised version of the case study at least two weeks before the review meeting. Any special instructions regarding confidentiality of the information should be provided as well as directions on how the reviewer is to provide feedback (in writing, by telephone, in a meeting). A meeting is held to have the review panel members provide three levels of feedback regarding the study (Lincoln and Guba, 1985): a judgment of the case study's overall credibility, statements about major concerns or issues, and statements about factual or interpretive error.

In reviewing the feedback, factual errors must be corrected. Where interpretive errors are concerned, the researcher cannot assume that the checkers are right and the researcher is wrong. It is possible that the reactions are the result of fronts or delusions. Each issue must be seriously considered and a decision must be made by the researcher regarding the revisions. In a case written by one of the authors, the researcher allowed a principal to have an addendum to the report stating his views and reactions.

Evaluating a Case Study Report

A naturalistic study is evaluated in terms of the quality criteria that were explicated in Chapter 7. A study must be judged in terms of its trustworthiness, authenticity, and ethical treatment of the stakeholders in the context being studied. As noted previously, one group of these quality criteria (the trustworthiness criteria) are methodological and parallel those that would be used in a conventional study. In addition to these criteria, however, the naturalistic researcher can also examine the process to see if it has been faithful to the tenets of the naturalistic paradigm. To accomplish this, the study may be evaluated to determine how closely it paralleled the hermeneutic-dialectic process described in Chapter 6. This process, with its immediate and continuing interplay of information and the continuous and multiple challenges from respondents, guards against the likelihood of noncredible outcomes. The lack of secrecy, given the public inspecta-bility of the process and products, prevents the biases of the evaluator or others from shaping the report.

Of even greater importance in determining the quality of a naturalistic study are the application of the authenticity criteria and the evidence of proactive application of ethics in the study. These criteria emanate from the naturalistic paradigm itself and the value it places on the free and informed interaction of separate constructions, and they are not parallel to anything required in a traditional study. The case study report must give evidence that it has accomplished the following:

- solicited and honored the constructions of the various stakeholders
- continually renegotiated the informed consent of the stakeholders
- developed stakeholders' understanding of their own constructions and others
- facilitated the translation of these consensual constructions into concrete plans, and
- empowered stakeholders to become origins of action in their social context.

In addition to safeguarding the stakeholders from harm in a more proac-tive way than that envisioned by conventional research methodology, the report of the study should also demonstrate that stakeholders have been empowered, educated, and connected with the constructions of other stake-holders in the social context to promote a richer level of understanding and insight for all participants.

The External Audit

Once the final draft is complete, it is time for an external audit. The first task is to identify an auditor who is knowledgeable in naturalistic inquiry. To facilitate the initiation of the audit, the researcher will provide the auditor with an overview of the project's purpose and an introduction to the audit filing system that was established and maintained during the course of the inquiry. After researcher and auditor have reached an agreement about the scope, procedures, logistics, and report format, the auditor will prepare and implement a work program to determine the trustworthiness of the study and the report that communicates it. Schwandt and Halpern (1988) outline the elements of this work program as follows:

1. Assess confirmability.
   a. Assess whether findings are grounded in the data.
   b. Assess whether inferences are logical.
   c. Assess utility of category structure.
   d. Assess whether the evaluator accounted for discrepant data.
2. Assess dependability.
   a. Assess appropriateness of inquiry decisions and methodological shifts.
   b. Assess degree and incidence of investigator bias.
3. Review credibility.
   a. Review the design and implementation of credibility strategies.
   b. Review the impact of credibility strategies on methodological choices, data sources, and findings.

Following the completion of the audit, a letter of attestation is prepared, giving the purpose and goals of the audit, a discussion of the process used, and a summary of the findings regarding trustworthiness. A vita of the auditor that establishes the auditor's credentials to carry out audits should be included along with the auditor's signature and the date of the audit.

The reader who conducts a naturalistic study is encouraged to consult Schwandt and Halpern (1988) for a complete discussion of the elements and requirements of an audit.

Delivery of the Report

The delivered report should be in its final, bound form. In providing it to the key members of the stakeholding groups, it is not necessary to provide the artifacts, journals, or audit trail items because these have already been reviewed by the external auditor and the review panel.

It is important to determine who will review the case study first. In the Lightfoot portraits (1983), the headmasters and principals read them before they were published. In the Skipper study (1989), the principal and superintendent were given copies before other copies were distributed to teachers, students, and the school library. Lightfoot emphasizes that it is important to make clear what expectations one has from these first readers. She told the principals in her studies that she was eager to hear their reactions, and she wanted corrections to any factual errors. One principal interpreted her request as an invitation for "dialogue." While he did not claim the portrait was untrue or unfair, he was afraid that it was too sharp and showed the teachers in a way they rarely were seen by the community. He wanted adjustments in several paragraphs. Lightfoot realized that she had given the principal mixed messages and had not made it clear whether she was inviting his collaboration or whether she simply wanted him to comment on the finished document.

In the Skipper (1989) study, there was a flurry of mumbling regarding a part of the study that said the school had little new blood and no internal criticism. When confronted as to whether this was an accurate portrayal, one teacher said, "Just because it is true doesn't make it easier to read!" The researcher must not be overly sensitive to such seemingly critical statements.

Lightfoot (1983, pp. 377-378) gives several lessons she learned regarding the challenges of such research:

- The investigator must be conscious of the affective dimensions of the work because it contains both ideas *and* emotions.
- The investigator should give careful attention to the research aftermath; the research exit is just as important as the research entry.
- There seem to be anticipative stages of reactions, from "terror" of exposure to denial to acceptance, that people experience when they read the study.
- The social scientist engaged in naturalistic research should recognize the potential impact of the work on individuals and institutions.

Some Alternative Formats

It was suggested at the beginning of the chapter that the report of a naturalistic inquiry is necessarily a work of art and that the format it takes should be most effective in enabling cognitive and emotional interaction between the context described and the intended audience. Every artist who would use words (as we most certainly do in reporting our studies) to link people and settings with an audience recognizes, at least intuitively, that the very nature of language as a classifying, simplifying, and stratifying device imposes certain distorting restrictions on communication. It is the art of the author, the playwright, or the poet that overcomes these limitations. Consider, for example, which best communicates, in both a cognitive and an emotional sense, the involvement of the United States in the Vietnam conflict: (1) a statistical report of the number of men and casualities, (2) the film *Apocalypse Now*, or (3) the Vietnam Memorial in Washington, DC? The answer to this question will differ from individual to individual, but all should agree that the impact of each example will be different. It is the task of the writer of the naturalistic inquiry research report to consider carefully the intended audience and the proposed impact on that audience.

It is not entirely clear what this line of reasoning means for the report of a naturalistic inquiry; at the very least it suggests that its format must be carefully chosen and shaped. One alternative format is that proposed by Lutz and Iannaccone (1969). This alternative builds what is essentially a case study into an overall format that is very close to that typically found in dissertation research. As such it may provide direction for the doctoral student whose dissertation committee is skeptical about naturalistic inquiry. Another possible format is the chart essay, described by Haensly, Lupkowski, and McNamara (1987). This format, directed to groups of busy policy makers and practitioners, combines oral and written presentations in a way that focuses the audience's attention on the relevant aspects of a study.

Ethnologists have used the case study in a variety of ways to communicate their constructed realities to their intended audiences. Greenhouse (1992) exemplified her overall national findings through the data she had collected and analyzed from the small suburban community of "Hopewell." In a parallel manner, Griffith, Valdás-Pizzini, and Johnson (1992) used the cases of six different individuals to illustrate the various aspects of their interpretation of proletarianization in the fisheries of Puerto Rico. As part of a larger, ethnographic study of home schools that he began in 1985, Knowles (1991) conducted in-depth studies of 12 home school families to gain understanding of the parents' rationales for operating those schools. In contrast to the typical survey strategies of previous studies, Knowles reported his findings through portraits of four local families that provided anecdotal evidence that he used to exemplify the parent rationales that he identified. Nash (1992) used her own interpretive analysis of the Bolivian resistance to economic conditions imposed by the International

Monetary Fund to demonstrate the need for supplementing textual interpretation with traditional methods of participant observation and the eliciting
of informants' own interpretations—a recognition of the need to deal with
the multivocalic complexity of human consciousness. These and other
studies illustrate well the flexibility of the case study in both its format
and ability to serve divergent purposes with divergent audiences. For this
reason we would urge the reader to regularly read the reports of studies
that are contained in journals such as *American Ethnologist, Human Organization, Journal of Contemporary Ethnography*, and *Qualitative Sociology*.
Through regular review of such studies, the aspiring naturalistic researcher
can learn much about the efficacy of varying formats for communicating
to various audiences.

Zeller (1987) analyzed alternative writing genres in terms of their
appropriateness for reporting cases. She recommends consideration of the
"nonfiction" novel, "new ethnography," and, particularly, "new journalism" as models for reporting a naturalistic study. The nonfiction novel is
typified by the writing of James Agee in *Let Us Now Praise Famous Men*
(Agee & Evans, 1988), an account that brings readers vividly into the lives
of three white tenant families in the South during the Great Depression.
New ethnography also brings the reader into the lives of the people,
departing from older ethnographic standards that emphasize objectivity.
Intimacy is not avoided in reporting, and the devices of the fiction writer
may be used to communicate the essence of the human setting. New
journalism, characterized by the writings of Tom Wolfe, emphasizes not
particular pieces of information, but the "scene," within which relationships are defined and particulars take on meaning. As Zeller notes, this is
very close to how the naturalistic researcher views the world and attempts
to analyze it. Zeller sees these three forms at the high point of a curvilinear
relationship between fiction and understanding, with the least fictional
(technical reports) and the most fictional forms (fable, allegory, and poetry)
being at the ends of the continuum that minimize understanding.

As naturalistic studies become more common, we hope that additional
reporting modes will also emerge. Though we thoroughly agree with
Zeller's purpose in establishing new reporting formats that better communicate the essence of a naturalistic study, we disagree that the forms on
the fictional end of her continuum cannot enhance this end. We believe that
several writers (Brooks, 1947; Wimsatt, 1954) have demonstrated well
that good poetry has the power to use words to overcome the abstracting,
stabilizing limitations of words and thereby enable the interpersonal communication of constructed realities that words would otherwise not permit.

We are impressed, for example, by the way in which poets such as Wordsworth, Keats, Frost, and Eliot have used words to overcome the limitations of words and to powerfully express subtle understandings and deep meanings not possible in prose. Perhaps poetry has possibilities for the naturalistic inquiry report, though we must admit that we do not know how strategies for providing trustworthiness (such as the audit trail) could be maintained! Nevertheless, we would encourage researchers who conduct naturalistic studies to envision and experiment with new formats that most effectively communicate the essence of the contexts they have studied.

Some Final Thoughts

According to Lightfoot (1983, p. 378) the "textured" form of a case study may serve as a catalyst for change within an institution. The external, "wide-angle view" may contrast sharply with the various perspectives of insiders; however, the dissonance provides opportunities for examining the roles and values of the organization.

In the Skipper study (1989), the principal of the school remarked that the researcher had learned in a short period of time what it took him six years to learn about the school. In some instances, the researcher provided the principal with information he had not yet synthesized about the system. The naturalistic inquiry process with its unfolding design, field problems, uneven reliability of data, and data overload still provides the most accurate, in-depth information in a relatively short time frame. This information can be used as a basis for identifying problems, facilitating change, or charting the school or organization's future directions.

The U.S. Department of Education's Office of Educational Research and Improvement sponsored *The Principal's Role in Shaping School Culture* by Deal and Peterson (1990), which used five case studies to analyze strategies for an effective principalship. The goal of the book was to encourage principals to reform their schools through shaping the school's culture. The case studies brought alive the ways five principals were able to weave academic excellence into the fabric of school life.

In fields such as anthropology, attention is now being turned to using the naturalistic inquiry process to study social problems such as family violence, teen pregnancy, drug abuse, civil war, and forest depletion. Anthropologists are beginning to find new ways of applying theories and findings to build better workplaces, improve social conditions, and market new commercial products. One anthropologist (Fleisher, 1989) not only completed a naturalistic study on life in a maximum security prison, but also used what he learned to write several training manuals that help guards understand and cope with the problems they confront. Much of the work in this field is reported in the Frontiers of Anthropology series (Sage Publications).

It is clear that in fields such as education, sociology, anthropology, and psychology the naturalistic study process is providing a means of exploring and understanding contexts—their successes, their issues, and their problems.

For Further Study

1. Prepare a tentative description and outline of the report format you will use for the naturalistic study you have been planning since Chapter 1. Explain why you have chosen this format.

2. Identify a study that has explicitly followed the naturalistic paradigm (e.g., Allen, 1990; Bifano, 1988; Harris, 1991; Skipper, 1989; Zeller, 1987). Prepare a written critique of how adequately the study has addressed its apparent audience, how well the reporting style serves the purpose of the inquiry, and how adequately it has met standards of trustworthiness and authenticity.

3. With a team of two or three other people conduct a naturalistic study. Possible organizations for study include shopping malls, schools, colleges within a university, hospitals, departments within a college of education, businesses, and so on. As a group, provide a presentation to an appropriate audience, including artifacts, raw data, journals, an audit trail, a summary of the organization's culture, and a reflective paper on what has been learned regarding the naturalistic inquiry process. *(Optional item)*

Afterword

THIS VOLUME BEGAN by offering to take the reader on an adventure in research. We hope that this objective has been accomplished. We hope also that the reader has developed a genuine appetite for exploring and analyzing social contexts. If this book has been successful, the reader will now have senses that have been sharpened to apprehend a wide range of contextual data, comprehension that has been broadened to formulate working hypotheses about that data, and thinking that has been disciplined to conduct a continuing analysis of that data. Most of all, we hope that the reader is inspired to continue to do naturalistic research that will make a difference in social settings.

We realize, of course, that naturalistic inquiry is not for everyone. Not everyone will be intrigued by the complexities of social settings; nor will everyone be willing to invest the time and energy that are necessary to make naturalistic inquiry successful. We hope that for these individuals we have at least explicated the requirements of what makes good naturalistic research and enabled them to read such research intelligently and critically. We will be satisfied if such individuals recognize the power of naturalistic inquiry and become eager consumers of it.

Even for a person who is inclined to do naturalistic research, the process can be a wearing and frustrating one. After completing her study of the attitudes held by community college faculty about adult students, Clark (1992) had these reflections:

The process is lengthy, time-consuming, and tends to lead one on [a] "wild goose chase." This researcher found that coding one interview could take as long as eight hours. There were 30 interviews, and each was coded several different times, resulting in what sometimes seemed an insurmountable task. It was very easy to become discouraged about ever finishing just this one part of the project. As coding progressed, there often seemed to be multiple avenues that needed to be explored, resulting in yet one more trip to the library.

Anyone considering such an undertaking must be able to conduct several different pieces, seemingly unrelated, of the project at the same time. This researcher found that review of literature, searches for sources for the goal statement, coding of interviews, analysis of literature, and analysis of interview coding [were] all going on at the same time. Each of these pieces played on other pieces so that at times it was necessary to put it all away for a while lest the researcher be overcome by the complexity.

Organization in such a project is essential. The mass of data collected takes up a great deal of physical space, and because the data [are] assimilated over a period of time, important pieces can get lost if a careful filing system is not maintained. It is fruitful to read over these files periodically in order to keep the final goal in mind and to remember what ground has already been covered. A common phenomenon in this type of research is to have a sudden flash of insight about the meaning of some bit of data; unfortunately, these "flashes" tend to recur. It is very important to record in some fashion journal notes and comments. This researcher has an interesting collection of used envelopes, paper napkins, credit card receipts, and miscellaneous notepads with vitally important bits of information; a better way would be to carry a small notebook or tape recorder just for this purpose.

This researcher cannot imagine having completed this project without the aid of the computer. She was able to relegate such mindless tasks as sorting to a computer program, thus being able to use her time and effort more efficiently. In addition, the computer doesn't miss a word or phrase because it is two o'clock in the morning. (pp. 177-179)

For either the prospective researcher or consumer of research we would offer a similar prescription for growth: Continue to read and analyze good naturalistic studies. In this book we have focused the reader's attention on a few excellent studies. There are many others. We would encourage the reader to search these out and read them. We would also encourage the reader to regularly follow several journals that emphasize qualitative research. The regular critical analysis of good research is a sound strategy for developing the skills of both the researcher and the consumer of research. The regular opportunity to compare and evaluate alternative research designs, data collection techniques, and analysis strategies is an exercise that provides both enjoyment and sharpened research skills.

The prospective naturalistic researcher also should be sensitive to significance in social settings. Such sensitivity is not acquired quickly; it is usually built on a lifetime of involvement with significant social issues. However, we think it is likely that the individual who has acquired enthusiasm for naturalistic research has already developed some sensitivity to social issues. This sensitivity, at whatever level, can be nurtured by regularly staying up with events in general or in a given field (e.g., by subscribing to *Education Week*) and by regularly reading or listening to social commentary.

Above all, we would recommend to the prospective naturalistic researcher that he or she not put off getting involved in a significant piece of research. The final "For Further Study" item in Chapter 8 suggested that a research team be found to pursue a naturalistic study. Or the study that the reader has designed while going through this text can now be implemented. Such a study may have been designed for dissertation research or for some other purpose. However, whatever the purpose of the study, whether it is planned as a team or as an individual piece of research, we would encourage the researcher to get started now—while enthusiasm is high and sensitivities are attuned to the requirements of good research. Once into the study, we trust that involvement in the social context will carry the researcher along for the most part. However, should natural interpersonal curiosity ever lose its holding power, we would use the words of Louis Agassiz to encourage the faltering researcher: "Look at your fish!" If new discoveries can stimulate fresh interest in a dead, soggy, smelly lower-order vertebrate, we are certain that fresh insights about dynamic social relationships can fuel the researcher's motivation to complete a significant naturalistic study.

References

Agee, J., & Evans, W. (1988). *Let us now praise famous men*. Boston: Houghton Mifflin.

Allen, S. D. (1990). *Principal-teacher interactions in urban high schools: Two case studies*. Unpublished doctoral dissertation, Texas A&M University, College Station, TX.

Bauer, R. L. (1992). Changing representations of place, community, and character in the Spanish Sierra del Caurel. *American Ethnologist, 19*(3), 571-589.

Bifano, S. L. (1987). *Elementary principals: Espoused theory and professional practice*. Unpublished doctoral dissertation, Texas A&M University, College Station, TX.

Bifano, S. L., & Erlandson, D. A. (1989). *The use of photographs in creating cultural profiles*. Paper presented at annual conference of the American Educational Research Association, San Francisco.

Boelen, W. A. (1992). Street corner society: Cornerville revisited. *Journal of Contemporary Ethnography, 21*(1), 11-51.

Bogdan, R. C. (1972). *Participant observation in organizational settings*. Syracuse, NY: Syracuse University Center on Human Policy.

Bogdan, R. C., & Biklen, S. K. (1982). *Qualitative research for educators*. Boston: Allyn & Bacon.

Bogdan, R. C., & Taylor, S. J. (1975). *Introduction to qualitative research methods*. New York: John Wiley.

Borg, W. R., & Gall, M. D. (1983). *Educational research: An introduction*. New York: Longman.

Brooks, C. (1947). *The well wrought urn: Studies in the structure of poetry*. New York: Reynal & Hitchcock.

Bruyn, S. (1966). *The human perspective in sociology: The methodology of participant observation*. Englewood Cliffs, NJ: Prentice-Hall.

Bryson, B. (1990). *Mother tongue: English and how it got that way*. New York: William Morrow.

Chace, P. G. (1992). Interpretive restraint and ritual tradition: Marysville's Festival of Bok Kai. *Journal of Contemporary Ethnography, 21*(2), 226-254.

Clark, S. H. (1992). *Community college faculty attitudes about adult students: Implications for faculty development.* Unpublished doctoral dissertation, Texas A&M University, College Station, TX.

Deal, T. E., & Peterson, K. (1990). *The principal's role in shaping school culture.* U.S. Department of Education. Washington, DC: Government Printing Office.

Denzin, N. K. (1970). *The research act: A theoretical introduction to sociological methods.* Hawthorne, NY: Aldine.

Denzin, N. K. (1987). *The alcoholic self.* Newbury Park, CA: Sage.

Denzin, N. K. (1992). Whose Cornerville is it, anyway? *Journal of Contemporary Ethnography, 21*(1), 120-132.

Dexter, L. A. (1970). *Elite and specialized interviewing.* Evanston, IL: Northwestern University Press.

Dingwall, R., Eekelaar, J., & Murray, T. (1983). *The protection of children: State intervention and family life.* Padstow, UK: T. J. Press.

Durst, P. L., Wedemeyer, N. V., & Zurcher, L. A. (1985). Parenting partnerships after divorce: Implications for practice. *Social Work, 30*(5), 423-428.

Eisner, E. W. (1985). *The educational imagination: On the design and evaluation of educational programs* (2nd ed.). New York: Macmillan.

Eisner, E. W. (1992). Are all causal claims positivistic? A reply to Francis Schrag. *Educational Researcher, 21*(5), 8-9.

Erickson, F. (1992). Why the clinical trial doesn't work as a metaphor for educational research: A response to Schrag. *Educational Researcher, 21*(5), 9-11.

Erlandson, D. A. (1979). Language, experience, and administrative preparation. *Planning and Changing, 10*(3), 150-156.

Erlandson, D. A. (1992). The power of context. *Journal of School Leadership, 2*(1), 66-74.

Fetterman, D. M. (1989). *Ethnography: Step by step.* Applied Social Research Methods Series, Vol. 17. Newbury Park, CA: Sage.

Fleisher, M. L. (1989). *Warehousing violence.* Newbury Park, CA: Sage.

Freedman, S. G. (1991). *Small victories.* New York: Harper-Collins.

Gage, N. L. (1989). The paradigm wars and their aftermath: A "Historical" sketch of research on teaching since 1989. *Educational Researcher, 18*(7), 4-10.

Gallaher, A. (1961). *Plainville fifteen years later.* New York: Columbia Unversity Press.

Gans, H. J. (1967). *The Levittowners: Ways of life and politics in a new suburban community.* New York: Pantheon.

Gans, H. J. (1982). *The urban villagers: Group and class in the life of Italian-Americans.* New York: Free Press.

Geertz, C. (1983). *Local knowledge.* New York: Basic Books.

Glaser, B. G. (1965). The constant comparative method of qualitative anlaysis. *Social Problems, 12*, 436-445.

Glaser, B. G., & Strauss, A. L. (1967). *The discovery of grounded theory.* Hawthorne, NY: Aldine.

Goodall, J. (1990). *Through a window.* Boston: Houghton Mifflin.

Greenhouse, C. J. (1992). Signs of quality: Individualism and hierarchy in American culture. *American Ethnologist, 19*(2), 233-254.

Griffith, D., Valdäs-Pizzini, M., & Johnson, J. (1992). Injury and therapy: Proletarianization in Puerto Rico's fisheries. *American Ethnologist, 19*(1), 53-74.

Guba, E. G. (1978). *Toward a methodology of naturalistic inquiry in educational evaluation.* Monograph 8. Los Angeles: UCLA Center for the Study of Evaluation.

Guba, E. G. (1981). Criteria for assessing the trustworthiness of naturalistic inquiries. *Educational Communication and Technology Journal, 29,* 75-92.

Guba, E. G. (Ed.). (1990). *The paradigm dialog.* Newbury Park, CA: Sage.

Guba, E. G., & Lincoln, Y. S. (1981). *Effective evaluation.* San Francisco: Jossey-Bass.

Guba, E. G., & Lincoln, Y. S. (1989). *Fourth generation evaluation.* Newbury Park, CA: Sage.

Habenstein, R. W. (Ed.). (1970). *Pathways to data: Field methods for studying ongoing social organizations.* Hawthorne, NY: Aldine.

Haensly, P. A., Lupkowski, A. E., & McNamara, J. F. (1987). The chart essay: A strategy for communicating research findings to policy makers and practitioners. *Educational Evaluation and Policy Analysis, 9,* 63-75.

Harris, E. L. (1991). *Identifying integrated values education approaches in secondary schools.* Unpublished doctoral disseration, Texas A&M University, College Station, TX.

Haworth, G. O. (1984). Social work research, practice, and paradigms. *Social Service Review, 58*(3), 349-357

Hayakawa, S. I. (1978). *Language in thought and action.* Orlando, FL: Harcourt Brace Jovanovich.

Heineman, M. B. (1981). The obsolete scientific imperative in social work research. *Social Service Review, 55*(3), 371-397.

Helmer, J. (1991). The horse in backstretch culture. *Qualitative Sociology, 14*(2), 175-195.

Hodson, R. (1991). The active worker: Compliance and autonomy at the workplace. *Journal of Contemporary Ethnography, 20*(1), 47-48.

Hofstadter, D. R. (1979). *Gödel, Escher, Bach: An eternal golden braid.* New York: Vintage.

Hollingshead, A. (1975). *Elmtown's youth and Elmtown revisited.* New York: John Wiley.

Jackson, T. F. (1991). *Development of a training and support program for older custodial and landscape workers.* Unpublished record of study proposal, Texas A&M University, College Station, TX.

Jackson, T. F. (1992, April 23). Interview.

Jacobs, J. (1991). New ethnographies: Warehousing violence. *Journal of Contemporary Ethnography, 20*(1), 114-119.

Jarvie, I. C. (1982). The problem of ethical integrity in participant observation. In Burgess, R. G. (Ed.), *Field research: A sourcebook and field manual* (pp. 68-72). Boston: Allyn & Bacon.

Johnson, J. M. (1975). *Doing field research.* New York: Free Press.

Keller, H. (1954). *The story of my life.* Garden City, NY: Doubleday.

Kerlinger, F. N. (1973). *Foundations of behavioral research* (2nd ed.). New York: Holt, Rinehart & Winston.

Kidder, T. (1990). *Among school children.* New York: Aron.

Klint, K. A. (1988). *An analysis of the positivistic and naturalistic paradigms for inquiry: Implications for the field of sport psychology.* Unpublished doctoral dissertation, University of Oregon, Eugene, OR.

Knowles, J. G. (1991). Parents' rationales for operating home schools. *Journal of Contemporary Ethnography, 20*(2), 203-230.

Korzybski, A. (1958). *Science and sanity: An introduction to non-Aristotelian systems and general semantics.* Lakeville, CT: International Non-Aristotelian Library.

Krathwohl, D. R. (1985). *Social and behavioral science research.* San Francisco: Jossey-Bass.

Kuhn, T. S. (1970). *The structure of scientific revolutions* (2nd ed.). Chicago: University of Chicago Press.

Lawrence, E. (1982). *Rodeo.* Chicago: University of Chicago.

Lidz, V. (1991). The sense of identity in Jewish-Christian families. *Qualitative Sociology, 14*(1), 77-102.

Lightfoot, S. L. (1983). *The good high school.* New York: Basic Books.

Likert, R. (1967). *The human organization: Its management and value.* New York: McGraw-Hill.

Lincoln, Y. S. (1989). Trouble in the land: The paradigm revolution in the academic disciplines. In J. C. Smart (Ed.), *Higher education: Handbook of theory and research* (Vol. 5, pp. 57-133). New York: Agathon.

Lincoln, Y. S. (1990). Toward a categorical imperative for qualitative research. In E. Eisner & A. Peshkin (Eds.), *Qualitative inquiry in education: The continuing debate.* New York: Columbia University Teacher's College Press.

Lincoln, Y. S., & Guba, E. G. (1985). *Naturalistic inquiry.* Beverly Hills, CA: Sage.

Lortie, D. C. (1975). *Schoolteacher: A sociological study.* Chicago: University of Chicago Press.

Loseke, D. R. (1992). *The battered woman and shelters: The social construction of wife abuse.* Albany: State University of New York Press.

Lutz, F. W., & Iannaccone, L. (1969). *Understanding educational organizations: A field study approach.* Columbus, OH: Charles E. Merrill.

Maril, R. L. (1983). *Texas shrimpers: Community, capitalism, and the sea.* College Station, TX: Texas A&M University Press.

Marshall, C., & Rossman, G. B. (1989). *Designing qualitative research.* Newbury Park, CA: Sage.

Martens, R. (1987). Science, knowledge, and sport psychology. *The Sport Psychologist, 1*(1), 29-55.

McCall, G. J., & Simmons, J. L. (Eds.). (1989). *Issues in participant observation.* New York: Random House.

McCarthy, M. J. (1991). *Mastering the information age.* Los Angeles: J. P. Tarcher.

McCrimmon, J. M. (1968). *From source to statement.* Boston: Houghton Mifflin.

McNamara, J. F., Fetsco, T. G., & Barona, A. (1986). Data-based debates: A strategy for constructing classification systems to report questionnaire data. *Public Administration Quarterly, 10*(3), 336-359.

Mead, G. (1934). *Mind, self, and society.* Chicago: University of Chicago Press.

Merriam, S. B. (1988). *Case study research in education: A qualitative approach.* San Francisco: Jossey-Bass.

Miles, M. B., & Huberman, M. (1984). *Qualitative data analysis: A sourcebook of new methods.* Beverly Hills, CA: Sage.

Mobley, C. C. (1991). *Interaction between diabetes educators and clients of low socioeconomic status: A naturalistic study.* Unpublished dissertation proposal, Texas A&M University, College Station, TX.

Mobley, C. C. (1992, April 28). Interview.

Murphy, M. D., & Johannsen, A. (1990). Ethical obligations and federal regulations in ethnographic research and anthropological education. *Human Organization, 49*(2), 127-134.

Nash, J. (1992). Interpreting social movements: Bolivian resistance to economic conditions imposed by the International Monetary Fund. *American Ethnologist, 19*(2), 275-293.

Patton, M. Q. (1980). *Qualitative evaluation methods.* Beverly Hills, CA: Sage.

184   DOING NATURALISTIC INQUIRY

Patton, M. Q. (1990). *Qualitative evaluation and research methods*. Newbury Park, CA: Sage.

Pennartz, P. J. (1989). Semiotic theory and environmental evaluation: A proposal for a new approach and a new method. *Symbolic Interaction, 12*(1), 231-249.

Peters, T. J., & Waterman, R. H., Jr. (1982). *In seach of excellence*. New York: Warner.

Piaget, J. (1950). *The psychology of intelligence*. London: Routledge & Kegan Paul.

Popkewitz, T. S. (1984). *Paradigm and ideology in educational research: The social functions of the intellectual*. New York: Falmer.

Popkewitz, T. S. (1992). Cartesian anxiety, linguistic communism, and reading texts. *Educational Researcher, 21*(5), 11-15.

Richardson, L. (1992). Trash on the corner: Ethics and technography. *Journal of Contemporary Ethnography, 21*(1), 103-119.

Schrag, F. (1992). In defense of positivist research paradigms. *Educational Researcher, 21*(5), 5-8.

Schwandt, T. A., & Halpern, E. S. (1988). *Linking auditing and metaevaluation*. Newbury Park, CA: Sage.

Schwartz, P., & Ogilvy, J. (1979). *The emergent paradigm: Changing patterns of thought and belief*. Analytical Report 7, Values and Lifestyles Program. Menlo Park, CA: SRI International.

Seidel, J. V., Kjolseth, R., & Seymour, E. (1988). *The Ethnograph: A user's guide*. Littleton, CO: Quolis Research Associates.

Seymour, D. T. (1988). *Marketing research: Qualitative methods for the marketing professional*. Chicago: Probus.

Shapira, R., & Navon, D. (1991). Alone together: Public and private dimensions of a Tel-Aviv cafe. *Qualitative Sociology, 14*(2), 107-125.

Sizer, T. R. (1984). *Horace's compromise: The dilemma of the American high school*. Boston: Houghton Mifflin.

Skipper, B. L. (1989). *The influence of culture at Randolph High School on teachers and students: A naturalistic study*. Unpublished record of study, Texas A&M University, College Station, TX.

Smith, L. M. (1990). Ethics in qualitative field research: An individual perspective. In E. Eisner & A. Peshkin (Eds.), *Qualitative inquiry in education: The continuing debate* (pp. 258-276). New York: Columbia University Teacher's College Press.

Soltis, J. F. (1990). The ethics of qualitative research. In E. Eisner & A. Peshkin (Eds.), *Sociological methods: A sourcebook*. Hawthorne, NY: Aldine.

Spier, L. (Ed.). (1941). *Language, culture, and personality: Essays in memory of Edward Sapir*. Menasha, WI: Memorial Publication Fund.

Spradley, J. P. (1979). *The ethnographic interview*. New York: Holt, Rinehart & Winston.

Strauss, A. L., & Corbin, J. M. (1990). *Basics of qualitative research: Grounded theory procedures and techniques*. Newbury Park, CA: Sage.

Swisher, K. (1986). Authentic research: An interview on the way to the ponderosa. *Anthropology and Education Quarterly, 17*, 185-188.

Taylor, S. J., & Bogdan, R. (1984). *Introduction to qualitative research methods: The search for meanings*. New York: John Wiley.

Taylor, V. (1992). *Social exchange in bureaucracies: A study in negotiating access to a business environment*. Unpublished doctoral dissertation, Texas A&M University, College Station, TX.

Tesch, R. (1990). *Qualitative research: Analysis types and software tools.* Bristol, PA: Falmer.

Vidich, A. J. (1992). Boston's North End. *Journal of Contemporary Ethnography, 21*(1), 80-102.

Whorf, B. L. (1956). *Language, thought, and reality: Selected writings of Benjamin Lee Whorf.* Cambridge: MIT Press.

Whyte, W. F. (1943). *Street corner society.* Chicago: University of Chicago Press.

Wilmore, B. E. (1988). *The establishment of criteria for standards of principal performance.* Unpublished doctoral dissertation, Texas A&M University, College Station, TX.

Wimsatt, W. K. (1954). *The verbal icon: Studies in the meaning of poetry.* Lexington: University of Kentucky Press.

Witters-Churchill, L. J. (1988). *University preparation of the school administrator: Evaluations by Texas principals.* Unpublished doctoral dissertation, Texas A&M University, College Station, TX.

Wolcott, H. F. (1973). *The man in the principal's office.* New York: Holt, Rinehart & Winston.

Yeager, P. C., & Kram, K. E. (1990). Fielding hot topics in cool settings: The study of corporate ethics. *Qualitative Sociology, 13*(2), 127-148.

Yin, R. K. (1984). *Case study research: Design and methods.* Applied Social Research Methods Series, Vol. 5. Beverly Hills, CA: Sage.

Zelditch, M., Jr. (1970). Some methodological problems of field studies. In N. K. Denzin (Ed.), *Sociological methods: A sourcebook.* Hawthorne, NY: Aldine.

Zeller, N. C. (1987). *A rhetoric for naturalistic inquiry.* Unpublished doctoral dissertation, Indiana University, Bloomington, IN.

Index

About the Authors

David A. Erlandson (Ed.D., University of Illinois, 1969) is Professor of Educational Administration at Texas A&M University. Before coming to Texas A&M University in 1977, he served on the faculty of Queens College, City University of New York, for 6 years and served for 11 years as a public school teacher and administrator in Illinois. He currently chairs the National Association of Secondary School Principals' University Consortium on Performance-Based Preparation of Principals. His research and development activities focus on the professional development of principals and on the restructuring of school environments. He is the author of *Strengthening School Leadership* (1976) and numerous journal articles related to the preparation and job requirements of the principal.

Edward L. Harris (Ph.D., Texas A&M University, 1991) is Assistant Professor of Educational Administration and Higher Education at Oklahoma State University. To that position he brought more than 15 years of experience as teacher and administrator. His current research and publication efforts focus on multiculturalism, values education, and school culture.

Barbara L. Skipper (Ed.D., Texas A&M University, 1989) is principal of Randolph High School on Randolph Air Force Base near San Antonio, Texas. She has spent more than 20 years in public education as a teacher, counselor, consultant, curriculum supervisor, and principal. In addition, she has taught at Incarnate Word College in San Antonio and written curriculum- and staff-development materials in the area of secondary mathematics. Her doctoral research provided a naturalistic case study that was based on a year of participant observation in a high school in Texas.

Steve D. Allen (Ph.D., Texas A&M University, 1990) is Director of Exceptional Education in the Alternative Schools of the Houston Independent School District. His doctoral research examined patterns of principal-teacher interaction in two urban high schools. His current research focuses on urban educational administration, administrative behavior, and the advancement of equal access for the inclusive community.